Changing Gears: Ups and Downs on the New Zealand Road is published under Catharsis Books, sectionalized division under Di Angelo Publications Inc.

CATHARSIS BOOKS

an imprint of Di Angelo Publications. Changing Gears: Ups and Downs on the New Zealand Road. Copyright 2018 Sequoia Schmidt in digital and print distribution in the United States of America.

Di Angelo Publications

4265 San Felipe #1100

Houston, Texas 77027 USA

www.diangelopublications.com

Library of Congress cataloging-in-publications data

Sequoia Schmidt. *Changing Gears: Ups and Downs on the New Zealand Road.* Downloadable via Kindle, iBooks, and NOOK.

Library of Congress Registration

Paperback

ISBN-10: 1-942549-18-0

ISBN-13: 978-1-942549-18-5

Layout: Di Angelo Publications

Cover Design: Di Angelo Publications

1.   Non Fiction Narrative —— Adventure ——Single Authored.
     United States of America with international distribution.

Changing Gears

*Ups and Downs on the
New Zealand Road*

Sequoia Schmidt

Author of:

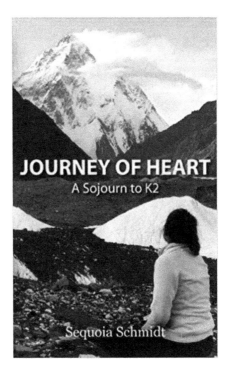

International Book Awards Finalist

Foreword
by Peter Hillary

This is a book about a homeland we share, New Zealand. Sequoia's observation is one of love for this country she was born in and wonder at the people, places, and history she discovers in her travels. It is also a book about courage. The courage one needs to face grief and troubles unflinchingly.

Sequoia and I have the heart-rending experience of suddenly losing a parent and sibling together in a tragic accident when we were in our early twenties. We were also born into adventurous families where mountaineering was featured as part of everyday life. We have the common experience of living on a daily basis without so many of those we love, of surviving. Surviving is often the most painful role to play in life.

One way to be in this world beyond mere survival is through confronting challenges and overcoming them. These challenges may be ones on the physical plane in meeting landscapes and dangers in nature, or on multifaceted, confusing inner landscapes where our aspirations, needs, questions, and memories merge, sometimes holding us back in fear.

I once stated: "If you don't know fear, then you haven't challenged yourself. And you haven't really   lived."

Sequoia Schmidt knows what fear is. She faces her fears and writes authentically about her experience in *Changing Gears: Ups and Downs on the New Zealand Road*.

DISCLAIMER

This book describes the author's experiences while cycling around New Zealand, and reflects her opinions relating to those experiences. Some names and identifying details of individuals mentioned in the book have been changed to protect their privacy.

South Pacific
Ocean

Tasman
Sea

Auckland

Hamilton   Tauranga

Rotorua

Taupo

Napier

Hawke's Bay

Palmerston North

Akatarawa Pass

Upper Hutt

Picton   Wellington

Blenheim

St Arnaud

The Rainbow Valley

Hanmer Springs

Waipara

Christchurch

N

W   E

S

najlakay

Chapter One

Quakes of Christchurch

"You can see where the fault line cracked it in half," David says as he points to the severed church, whose stone fragments are scattered to my feet. I could kick them if not for the divide of a mesh metal fence rusted with the emotions of 185 lives lost and seven long years since the earthquake struck. I have memories of hearing about the New Zealand earthquake. When it happened it seemed like a universe away, I had removed myself so far from Aotearoa and the painful memories of my past.

As David, Vicky, and I wander the paved streets of Christchurch, monuments of mourning for the lives of those lost in this devastating natural disaster are more evident. The quakes (there were two large ones and well over 10,000 aftershocks) greatly impacted the local community and the nation of New Zealand. We pause in front of a patch of green grass nestled between two dramatically contrasting structures. To the right, a brand new shiny and architecturally intriguing construction; apartments would be my guess. To the left are the remains of a broken office building, its debris an indicator of the horror that affected so many. My gaze returns to the grass in front of us. Raindrops from the inconsistent showers of the morning rest on the lush green blades of grass that outline the 5-meter by 5-meter stretch of oasis. One hundred and eighty-five white chairs sit alone, evenly spaced atop the greenery. One hundred and eighty-five chairs, symmetrically lined and perfectly eerie.

"What are they?" I ask.

"They are for the 185 people killed."

Vicky's voice is somber. One hundred and fifteen of them were trapped inside the CTV building when the biggest earthquake struck, including 26 young Japanese students simply searching for the new experiences and outlooks on life that they thought this small foreign country had to offer.

We begin to round the corner. I notice there are pictures, mementos, and some fresh flowers left by loved ones still mourning their losses seven years later.
Events become a lot more real when you are there to witness them in person, or simply witness the aftermath.

My father's last house was in Christchurch. If I remember correctly it was one of the many in Opawa damaged by the earthquake. My uncertainty in confirming the damage is because I simply do not know. My father was not a part of my life for a number of years. A fracture happened which caused me to retract my love and sever all contact.

At the time of the Christchurch earthquake, I was

in a world so disconnected from my past that this devastating natural disaster was simply a sound bite playing on the news in the breakroom while I poured coffee into a Styrofoam cup before returning to my office, far from Aotearoa.

New Zealand is like this earthquake to me. I am returning home for the first time in 10 years to face the painful memories which devastated me in the past. This is a chance to mourn in solitude and an opportunity to rebuild on the broken.

"It is sad that so much of the beautiful historic and Gothic architecture is gone," Vicky says, referring to a gargoyle-esque statue whose head and an arm are nowhere to be seen. The remnants remind me of the dark beauty of an old European city like Prague.

We begin the drive back to David and Vicky's house on the hill. They point out the "the new glass boxes," as Vicky calls them, referring to the modern buildings that occupy the dirt that once held the history of Christchurch.

"All this great history and great architecture are gone," I say, heartbroken. "Doesn't it frustrate you that this city is no longer what it once was?"

The car's engine noise covers a moment of silence before Vicky responds.

"You realize that it is the people who matter, the people who remain. That's what makes a city great."

I connected with Vicky and David while trekking in the Khumbu Valley of Nepal. As we wandered high in the Himalayas, something about their enthusiastic natures enchanted me. They met when they were just kids in high school, fell in love, and have experienced the joys that life offered them since then. They have two beautiful grown children, satisfying careers, a passion for exploration, and a stable home to welcome them after their travels. A beautiful life, one worthy of envy, and one that I'm not sure I will ever have. My nomadic spirit is too strong.

That evening, after I visited my family's old house (Not the same one my dad lived in), David begins to make dinner, spaghetti with the smell of stability. I take out my phone and show Vicky pictures of my afternoon activities. As we sit on the dark-green couch that lines the wall, running parallel to the wooden dining room table, I scroll through the photos displaying the street and home, a glimpse of a small part of my childhood in Christchurch.

"Who is that?" Vicky asks. She is pointing to a woman on my screen. This woman is in her early 60s, olive skin, blue eyes, and brown hair. Stern and sober, a face that has undoubtedly seen much in her lifetime. A delicate face. Weathered creases of grief line her eyes, and although she may appear joyful in the captured image, she resonates with the burden of longing, longing for what was lost. This is my mother. My mother who flew over from Afghanistan to meet me in Christchurch and show me the home in which I spent the first few years of my life. My mother,

13

whose motivations and ways of thought I have struggled to understand. My mother, who challenges me. My mother, whom I must balance a relationship with, using caution. But I do not answer Vicky with this complexity. Instead I simply say, "This is my mother." Vicky smiles and we continue scrolling.

"This tree was planted just a year and a half after I was born. My father brought a sapling over on a plane from California, back when you could fly things like that over on a plane." I chuckle. "Mum and Dad planted it in the yard of the home here in Christchurch right when we all moved down here in 1992. It's a sequoia. It's my sequoia tree."

On the screen in front of me is a picture of the outside of our former home on Grange Street. My mother and I are arm in arm, standing in front of a tall brown fence that lines the perimeter of the front garden. Towering above us, almost 12 meters (40 feet) tall, is a strong, healthy, and powerful redwood tree just a year and a half younger than I – putting my 157 centimeters (5'2") to shame.

"Dinner's ready," David calls from the kitchen. A warm delicious supper puts me right to sleep. An early morning devoted to sorting out my final gear is what I will face tomorrow.

Chapter Two

Preparation for the Known

It began on Venice Beach just six months before my plane touched down in New Zealand. The thought of returning to my homeland had been lingering in my mind for some time, but I knew that it was going to be an emotional mountain I was not quite ready to climb. So why now? What makes me ready? There is no definitive answer, no calculated therapeutic reckoning, no grand moment of realization. I simply woke up one morning and thought, *I would like to cycle around New Zealand.* Moments after that thought entered my mind I did one of the things I do best: I spontaneously spent a large chunk of money. I know what you are thinking... I am going to make a great wife some day. But this spontaneous purchase was actually one of the best things I have ever bought. It was plane ticket to New Zealand.

In reality, I purchased it for two reasons: one, because I knew that if I did not do this in that moment, I would continuously postpone my return; and two, I had a feeling that once I began the inevitable task of researching "long-distance solo cycle trips," there was a good chance I would find some fabulous excuse to back out.

However, if I had already purchased the plane ticket, it would force me to follow through on my commitment.

Thus, after my spontaneous acquisition, I began my research which led to the realization that I had no earthly idea what I was actually getting myself into.

"You are going to need to learn how to clip in!" my uncle Charlie said to me over Christmas dinner at his cabin in Bear Valley. *Clip in?* I thought. *What the heck is that?*

Uncle Charlie and Aunt Doris are avid cyclists who spend their free time cycling in the Swiss Alps and Dolomites (tough life). To my benefit, this meant that they had a wealth of knowledge when it came to cycling equipment. In the basement of their cabin, my well-prepared aunt and uncle used their stationary bike to demonstrate the process of clipping in. All looked well and easy.

"What brand of cycling shoes are you leaning toward?" my uncle inquired, his boyish enthusiasm for gear talk shining through.

"I have to get special shoes?" *Oh crap*, I thought. *This is going to cost a lot.*

My uncle sent a worried look in my aunt's direction.

Aunt Doris made her way to the closet next to the stationary bike and took out a series of cycling shoes.

"These are Pearl Izumi Elite. They are made for women, a solid, basic shoe with a standard clip-in," she said, holding up a pair of black clunky shoes with a Velcro strap and a large strip of metal covering the sole. She walked over to the stationary bike, space-tastic shoe in hand. She placed the metal at the bottom of the shoe in line with the pedal. Pressure slightly applied. Click. The shoe was now locked in place on the pedal of the bike.

"This is how the shoes clip in to a bike," she explained with a tone that brought me right back to when I was a pre-teen and could still defer to an elder's firm voice.

"So why do I have to clip in? Can't I just wear tennis shoes?" I sensed the stupidity of my question before it tumbled out of my mouth.

I could see Aunt Doris's worried look begin to create wrinkles. Uncle Charlie jumped in. "Because when you are riding all day, for consecutive days, your body will wear out. You want to make your riding as easy as possible on your body. Clipping in allows you to not drain too much energy. Preserving energy is vitally important for long rides, especially with hills."

Following that Christmas holiday week I was feeling a little more confident with my newfound knowledge of cycling shoes.

I entered the den of the mother hen: Bike Barn. This store lived up to its name. It was wall to wall with the latest and greatest cycling equipment. I snared a sales associate and explained my grandiose plan. She smiled at me and told me of her recent cycle from Canada to the States. She had the calf muscles to prove it.

"Right, then," she said with determination. "Let's start with a seat. We can measure your sit bones for this. You will also need pedals, shoes, helmet...."

"Oh, actually," I interrupted, "I am picking my helmet up in New Zealand." I felt pride in my preparedness. It was true, this part I had arranged. I found an excellent company online called Natural High. They specialized in New Zealand bike tours.

People from all over the world actually travel to New Zealand to cycle the country. Who knew? Apparently I am not the only lunatic out there. I spoke with Natural High's Christchurch manager and made arrangements to pick up the bike there and drop it off upon my arrival in Auckland 28 days later (fingers crossed I'm not road kill).

"Excellent," the saleswomen said. "You will need some gloves, cycling shorts, shoe covers, leg warmers," ... my brain started to hurt ... "arm covers, head band." The litany continued as I followed her around the store, dollar signs mounting.

"Oh, you must have some butt cream!"

"Some what?" I said with a look of amused astonishment.

"Butt cream. It's fantastic! Just rub it on your ass in the morning before your ride and it will prevent chafing."

"I am going to take your word for it," I said with a smirk.

I almost had a heart attack at the register when I saw the bill. The latest and greatest cycling equipment does not come cheap. Nine hundred dollars later, I was kicking myself for following through on my impulsive decision to cycle around New Zealand.

Purchasing the equipment was only the beginning of the preparation process. Hammering out the details is one of the single most important things we must do before any great adventure, and honestly, it is one of the most exciting parts, for we can only get ready so much based off of our known facts.

For example, provided nothing drastic occurs (knock on wood), I know that I will be cycling for approximately 50-100 kilometers a day (depending on the day) for a total of approximately 28 days (more or less). This trip will span sixteen cities across the two main islands of New Zealand, a portion of which will be spent off-road in the Rainbow Valley on the South Island. In case it has taken you a moment to clue in—this is a shitload of cycling.

Which brings us back to preparation; i.e., getting in shape through training.

One of Los Angeles's well-known features is the stretch of pavement linking Santa Monica, Venice, and a number of other popular beaches on the west shore. Thus my training began on a beach in Venice. I attempted to master the art of clipping in, or as I like to call it, "Satan's way of cycling". Upon reflection, I probably should have trained for clipping in on a stationary bike and not on a concrete path.

Balance has always come naturally to me, or so I thought. However, attempting to balance while clipped in as my bike came to a slowing point or standstill was next to impossible. You would think that the idea of hitting the pavement would serve as inspiration to learn the motions of a speedy unclip, but alas, rather the opposite occurred. An instant reaction kicks in to fight the ground coming toward you, causing your body to stick your hands out – instead of quickly unclipping.

It took me two and a half weeks of scrapes and bruises to master the art of clipping in and unclipping. I still get a giggle out of the concerned looks on my friends' faces when they would say things like, "You do have health insurance, right?"

Chapter Three

The Concept of Home

When you are asked to picture your childhood home, what is it that you imagine?
What is the color of the door?
How does the hallway look?
What is the smell in the kitchen?
Do you have an image of this dwelling that houses your childhood moments?
How crystal is your memory?

Mine is not. Mine is scattered, like the emotions of my youth. However, when I think of New Zealand and the memories that the small town of Hastings, Hawke's Bay holds for me, I think of my father's flat as my childhood home. Although my brother and I did not spend longer than three years in this house, and none of them consecutive, those years seem to be the most prominent memories of my youth in New Zealand. I wish I could say that they were all happy—many of them were—but unfortunately, the memories at the forefront of my mind hold anger and pain. As human beings, our recollections tend to focus on our scarring moments, sometimes supplanting our pleasant memories.

That is not to say that there were not moments, many moments, of joy, but simply to say that the fleeting memories of a happy childhood seem not to be as present or accessible. They will take more searching and recall.

I know that to return to this place still holding so much pain and anger will be to face my greatest fears in life. But I also know I want to do this. I am choosing to do this.

My life as of late has consisted of what others would call "becoming intimate with fear". My monthly recreational activities have encompassed what many presume to be some of the scariest and most dangerous things a person can experience in peacetime. Human flight, for example.

When I began training for my skydiving license, I touched a tippy-toe into another world of adventure, one of the many I have begun to explore. What I've found with these extreme sports is that we humans are capable of much more than we previously believed was possible. Thus I have ventured into the world of "the adventurers"—pushing my body and mind into the realm of the unlimited.

One of my most serious limitations, one of my greatest fears, has been to come face to face with the demons of pain, with my anger. I never thought I would be ready to decipher these kinds of emotions. I wasn't sure how to explore them. Now I know where to start.
I will start on a bike. I will start in Christchurch. I will start by putting one foot in front of the other.

Chapter Four

First-step Frustrations

My eyes open, glimpsing the first rays of morning light peering through large bay windows, revealing an ideal vantage point from the hill where David and Vicky make their home. The lack of an alarm clock's beep is a pleasant way to wake. I'm not quite sure if my early rising is because I am excited about the day ahead or if I am still moved by the energies of my recent climb.

Just four days ago my climbing partner, Iain, and I were waking up at 2 a.m. to begin our six-hour ascent of Mt. Aspiring's northwest ridge. Coming off a climb always leaves me a little high. I am caught in the euphoria of a summit with the intersection of the horizontal world. The last three days I rose in the wee hours of the morning in anticipation of the day's activities.

Today is no different. My morning will consist of a final pack, followed by a drop point and four to five hours of riding. Have I lost you? To break it down: I will spend the morning sorting out my gear, distinguishing my final needs from my wants, which can be a daunting task.

I step outside onto the charcoal-colored driveway leading to a small garage currently housing my 52-cm Surly Long Haul Trucker (type of bike). In case you are as lacking in your knowledge of bikes as I was, there are thousands of types out there. As a cyclist your bike swagger is partially determined by your style of ride. To give myself a confidence boost on the subject of cycling, when I am asked about my bike I say (in a cool, gear-talk tone), "I'm on a Surly." The said Surly will be my home on wheels for the next 28 days.

Collecting the bike from David and Vicky's garage, I lay it down on the pavement. Back to the garage I go, back and forth, back and forth, until in front of me on a blue tarp is a huge pile of the belongings which will be my only companions for this upcoming journey. This expedition will be a completely new experience for me. I have never cycled long distances before, and never been entirely solo. The excitement for my upcoming adventure is evident when I view the amount of supplies I have gathered. Unlike some of my previous escapades, I have actually trained for this trip. There is blood on the Venice Beach pavement to prove it.

I remind myself of this constantly as reassurance that my training did in fact take place. Venice Beach was my gateway drug and Mulholland Drive (a long winding road through the Los Angeles Hills) was my heroin.

I commence the process of spreading out my gear. I sort through the items and begin to pack them all in my big blue duffle bag. The duffle bag, along with half of my equipment, comes from Macpac, an outdoor outfitter which was one of my dad's main sponsors for his climbing expeditions. Prior to my arrival to New Zealand, I contacted this company to let them know my plans. They welcomed me to visit their headquarters and meet the many friendly faces who spent some time over a number of years with my father. He tested gear for them and helped to design new products.

Dad was loved by many people in the outdoor adventure community, and more specifically in the climbing community. New Zealand has numerous alpinists, both local and international, who reside in the South Island due to its spectacular training grounds.
Just a week before this packing task, I had the chance to experience the beauty of New Zealand's mountains firsthand.

Mt. Aspiring was one of the many climbs that my father used for training before heading to the Himalayas. It was a wonderful experience to share a hut with mountain guides who knew and respected my father. When I am venturing into the mountains, it is a badge of pride that I wear well, being the daughter of Marty Schmidt. That pride also carried over while touring the Macpac headquarters in Christchurch. Meeting people like Gavin, a tall, thin man who knew his way around equipment better than Peter Rabbit in a carrot patch. Gavin worked with my father on gear testing. Gavin would give Dad the latest advanced models of backpacks, jackets, tents, and sleeping bags, and Dad's job was to take pictures of them and test them out on climbs. Classic sponsorship. Photos of my father framed the hallway entrance to the Macpac headquarters, and numerous friendly faces greeted me with enchanting stories of Dad's pop-ins to the office.

Alex, the CEO, told me of the morning he was pulling into the parking lot "only to see Marty making coffee and eggs out of his van that he had obviously slept in." None of this surprised me, as it was classic Dad.

Like they did for my father's many expeditions, Macpac equipped me with an abundance of gear: rain jackets, shirts, gloves, mountain freeze-dried food – everything that was missing from my $900 shopping spree at Bike Barn. Between Macpac and Bike Barn, a wealth of gear was now packed in a blue duffle bag which would accompany me. *How?* you may ask. Why, that is a wonderful question. The exact question I asked just two months earlier when I was wondering how on earth I would manage to carry all of this equipment, along with a tent, stove, and sleeping bag, throughout my entire trip.

The answer lies in a trailer. A big beautiful trailer called the Y Large. I head back into David and Vicky's garage and carry out the large cardboard box which contains my trailer. "It will be easy to put together," I remember the representative of the biking trailer company telling me. "Just a few nuts and bolts."

A few nuts and bolts, my ass.

I unload the contents of the box onto the driveway, still damp from the morning dew. There are approximately 35 screws and bolts, along with multiple pieces of wood and two wheels. Given that Ikea furniture assembly perplexes me, you can only imagine what this sight is doing to my nerves. Unfolding the instructions, I begin the daunting task of assembling my Y Large trailer. To my surprise it goes faster than I expect.

"How's it coming out there?" David calls from the top of the wooden stairs that lead from the driveway to their front door.

"Fantastic. I've assembled the pile of frustration known as the Y trailer," I say, beaming with pride.

"Splendid," David replies, looking down at my creation. "So what's all that then?" He is pointing at a small pile of excess screws, a few pieces of wood, and a long hunk of metal.

"Never mind that," I reply hastily—confident bravado spurts from my mouth. "Concentrate on the beauty of my creation."

The fact is, my assembly closely resembles that which is pictured in the instructional package, so I am happy.
David chuckles and makes his way downstairs to help me as I begin to load my gear into his blue Subaru. It's a tight squeeze but we make it work by unhooking the tire from my bike.

With a big hug for Vicky, I say my farewells. David and I are off.

Last night we all decided it was best if David drove me to the outskirts of the city. The main motorway is the only real way to safely get out of

Christchurch, and they don't feel comfortable with me biking along that route. I gave in to their parental charms and agreed to have a drop point.

"Do you have your map?" David asks. I nod. "We will make sure to activate our Facebook account to watch your travels." David's paternal nature shines through.

Yes, you read that correctly. He said "our Facebook account," as in a shared account. It literally says "David and Vicky" on Facebook. Whenever I see it I giggle on the outside, but my independent nature screams at the thought of that kind of togetherness.

David and Vicky are a symbol for me, one of many couples in my life who represent the quintessential elements of "normal". I have Davids and Vickys all over the world. Older couples with whom I have formed close relationships.

My brother would often do the same thing. It's as if we both liked to be aligned to people who had "normal" lives as our touchstones, but at the same time retain the ability to fly solo. Perhaps I'll simply become a story that David and Vicky tell their friends about at dinner parties.

We reach the drop point outside of Christchurch. I say my goodbyes to dear David then spread my wings once more.

Chapter Five

From City to Scents

Not two minutes into my cycle and I notice that there is an inconsistent bouncing with my trailer—a terribly inconsistent bouncing which bothers me. There is also a strange sound accompanying the jagged bouncing. I see a gas station coming up on my left and ride my bike into the open space between the pumps and the shop.

I dismount, and not in the sexy way I've seen in movies where the hot blond dismounts the motorbike in one fluid motion, followed by an unveiling of her sun-kissed hair from the inner reaches of her sleek black helmet. No, that's far too sophisticated for me and my clipping bike. Instead, I barely make it off the bike in one piece. The act of clipping out upon stopping seems to have flown from my memory over the past two weeks. I have not been riding my bike, but traveling and climbing Mt. Aspiring.

Awkwardly disengaging from my bike grips, I begin to circle my cycle while attempting to diagnose the problem. There is it, simple as day— the mount attached to the cycle, which is supposed to align and connect perfectly with the hook from the trailer, is not aligned at all. In fact, it looks more like there is an entire section missing. Maybe dear David was right to question my assembly. Perhaps, just perhaps, one of those many bolts or screws would have made the difference.

There is not much I can do about my missing parts right now, as they are lying in a small pile in David and Vicky's garage.

Being a woman of the 21st century, I am sure I can figure this out. Besides, it's not like I am out of civilization just yet. I am parked in a gas station, for goodness sake.

Heading into the shop, I come to a halt by the tool section. It is equipped well enough to handle any car/bike malfunction. From the shelf I grab a reel of thick wire and a pair of wire cutters.

"Excuse me," I say to the attendant. He looks up from behind the counter with a mouth full of sausage roll.

"Do you think I could just cut a piece off of this reel?" Pause. "I will pay for the whole thing." There is an awkward silence, like he doesn't quite understand what I am asking.

"So you don't want the wire cutters?"

"No, I just need them to cut a little piece and then I will put them straight back. You can even have the rest of the reel."

"Uhhhh. Sure?" he replies, still a little confused.

"Thanks." I cut a piece off and then head to the counter to pay. "Light is right, you see."

"What?"

"Traveling light is the right way to travel. I am on a bicycle, trying to cycle the country, so I need to travel without any extra weight."

"$2.50," he says with a blank stare.

He couldn't care less about my cycle ride. I am obviously far more excited about this trip than he is. He has no part in it so why should he be excited about my 28-day, two-wheel journey, of which I have completed exactly two minutes so far?

I wonder if this over-enthusiasm will fade. I wonder if by Day 15 I will no longer feel the need to tell a shop keeper about my #cyclegoals.

I return to my bike and feed the thick wire through the hook hole which attaches my bike to my trailer. I have enough extra coil to wrap it around three to four times and then twist the ends to fasten tightly.

Bouncing the bike a few times to make sure the hook and mount are in perfect alignment. Next, I walk the bike a few steps to make sure the bouncing has stopped.

Finally, I am ready to mount my bike un-sexily by clipping in my right foot while the rotation of the pedal is at its high point. Placing pressure on the right foot, I clip in my left and I'm off.

A feeling of pride flows through me. Not only am I back on my bike, continuing my journey, but I resolved my first issue.

Approximately 15 kilometers later, a short glance in my helmet mirror shows me that the gas stations have faded in the distance. Paved entrances, side streets, and shops have transitioned to the motorway bordered by grass-filled gullies leading to farms and grazing pastures. I am headed into the country and have officially left the city behind.

There is a certain smell that the countryside of New Zealand has, scents I have not smelled in a long time. This smell energizes me. This smell propels me forward. I am not quite sure how to describe this aroma. I would equate it to trying to describe the act of being in love. It's not easily definable in a word or phrase. The definition and description may vary depending on whom you ask.

In one word, the smell of New Zealand's countryside is "fresh". Not a very inventive word, I know. But I think it's descriptive and evocative.

With the influx of fresh in my nostrils and a light breeze picking up behind me, the circular movement becomes more natural. A rhythm is forming. A rhythm which will allow me to keep a steady pace for the next few hours. This rhythm is something I have to create on my own since there is no music in my ears.

Many people told me I was crazy for not bringing music to listen to on my long ride. But hear me out because I believe my logic is sound. Although music can be my motivation, it can also be a distraction. New Zealand roads are *known to not be* the most suitable for cycling. Approximately 12 cyclists per year are killed on the winding roads (according to the NZ Transport Agency). That may not sound like a lot, but for a country with only 268,021 km² and 4.6 million people—of which 19% ride bikes—it's actually quite significant.

There are many reasons for this – poor drivers may be one, narrow roads with no cycle lanes may be another. Yet one thing is for certain: if I want to come out of these 28 days without too much damage, I should stay as alert as possible. I want to be able to hear the cars coming up behind me, to have my senses fully alert. To allow my mind to be clear. Hence, no music.

Chapter Six

Grapes of Wrath

One of the hardest things about doing something solo is the self-motivation it takes to complete it. It comes naturally to some people. I am not one of those people. My natural tendency is to want to pull over to the grass coming up because my legs hurt and although I have been peddling for only two hours, it feels like 20. My natural tendency is to complain… even if my complaints simply echo in my own ears.

Sometimes I complain aloud in the hopes that my own whining will annoy me so much that I will be inspired to shut myself up and keep riding. Or sometimes, like today, my complaints cause me to pull my bike over to the side of the empty motorway, rest the pedal against a solid-wood picket fence holding a vine of lush grapes, and take a knee in the grassy shade as a sweet burst of New Zealand's finest grapes enters my mouth.

Lying in the shadow of a large tree, an abundance of earthy grapes satisfying my stomach, I look up to see frothy white clouds.

As a little girl, I used to watch clouds, picking out the passing shapes. I would draw comfort from them. They were some constants in my ever-changing environments. Now as I look up at a dome of clouds, my mouth filled with the lingering taste of sweet grapes, memories flood to my mind. Memories of Hawke's Bay and the ghosts who linger in the columns of vineyards.

I was in this moment before.
Sixteen years ago.
I was in this moment before.

My belly full of grapes, my eyes on the clouds. Fixated on the clouds, searching for stability.

"Young lady!"

I can still hear the CYFS officer calling my name. The Child Youth and Family Services officer became a familiar voice in my ear.

"Young lady" seemed to be my category, a category that was now my name.

"Young lady, this is not behavior that is tolerated." Maybe if I didn't make a sound I would turn to stone and the world could forget my existence.

"Young lady, we do not run away from our problems." He obviously didn't know this young lady very well.

By the age of 10, I had become a master of running away from my problems. CYFS officer #1 pulled me out of class to inform me that the Martins family would no longer be my temporary caregivers and I would have to return to my mother's house in Te Awanga.

My solution? Run. Run… for that is what I did best. Four gold trophies sat on a wooden shelf in the room at my mother's Te Awanga home. Proof of my speedy ability to escape.

Being pulled out of class was bad enough, but I was made to sit in a dark room with no natural light, no art on the walls, a stark office. I was told to sit in a stereotypical black stiff chair with my 10-year-old legs squirming. I can still smell the stench of authority.

As soon as CYFS Officer #1 turned his head, I was gone. I escaped and ran two kilometers down gravel roads into the vineyards.

"Young lady, present yourself," his persistent voice echoed over the pickets. *Present myself? This is not a court, and I am far from a princess.* Those thoughts still linger in my mind, as if it were yesterday that my mother was seen as unfit to provide a stable home due to allegations of her mental instability.

"I am just different, I think different, and people don't understand different," my mother used to tell us.

Sometimes at night I would crawl into my brother's bed to ask him why Mum was dressed all in black with green painted all over her face. Sometimes I would crawl into Denali's bed to ask him why Mum was chanting to Native American sundance music so loud it seemed to shake the house. Sometimes I would crawl into my big brother's bed just so he could reassure me that Mum wasn't crazy, that Mum was just different.

If Denali were there in the vineyards to reassure me, there would be no need to escape. But Denali had been taken in by a "not so temporary" caregiver. Denali always seemed to have welcoming arms. Why didn't I?

I know now.

It took me many years to figure it out. A total of 23 different "temporary families" before my 16th birthday. Twenty-three askings of "Why not me?"

In the beginning I would ask why everything seemed to come easily to Denali. Why people seemed to like Denali. Why this life seemed so natural to Denali. And why not me.

Toward the end of the 23 placements, I was too jaded to even ask. Too independent to question.

The truth is I had a fire inside of me. It started that day in that vineyard. A pile of small freshly cut kindling stacked neatly inside of me ignited sparks in the columns of that vineyard 16 years ago, and if not carefully maintained my small flames would burn, would blaze, and demolish everything in my path.

People were scared of my fire back then…so much fire in such a little girl. Back then, I didn't know how to control my fire. I let it run wild, leaving only ashes to my obstacles.

Sixteen years later, I am thankful for my fire. My inner flame may allow me a moment of reflection, but it also will burn me back onto my bike. My fire will burn under my feet until my legs can no longer sustain the circular motion that will propel me forward. My fire will burn and oh, my fire will blaze.

Even the smallest increases of elevation require so much energy. I have been on the road for three hours now, constant pedaling, constant pedaling. Every other kilometer calls me to change my body position. My sticky hands move from the top layer of my handlebars to the bottom moon-shaped mount.

"That's not what I trained on," I told the bloke who delivered my bike from Natural High.

"A multi-level handlebar—trust me, they are great." Boy, am I glad I trusted the biker bloke. I could kiss these moon-shaped handlebars.

The winds are starting to pick up. Suddenly I can feel every pound attached to my bike. It's like my trailer cheated on its Jenny Craig diet. Profanity projects from my mouth, but it doesn't quite reach my ears as the wind hollers. It is as if an invisible wall is forming in front of me.

"Pedal, pedal," I tell myself. "You got this, stay strong." A sting hits the back of my neck as the wind whips my hair. It feels as if I am hauling a truck. The harder I pedal, the heavier the truck becomes. The wind howls around me. I just have to make it past this small hill and I will be in the gully where the walls of the valley will block this wind.

Looking down at my watch, I'm moving a lot slower than I planned. I don't know if this is just my physical fitness or the fact that I feel like Nicki Minaj with this trailer on my ass.

I have to find a way to shed weight. There is no way I can keep going at this pace. I will never even make it to my first stop, Hanmer Springs.

When I was mapping out this section of the trip, Waipara was supposed to be my halfway point for the day, the spot where I could relax and have lunch before continuing onto Hanmer Springs. But as I push my pedals in their circular motion toward Waipara, the realization occurs that the halfway point was not even close. My energy is draining quickly.

My laziness is really kicking in now. There's a constant devil on my shoulder telling me to simply stick out my thumb. The problem with doing a solo trip in civilization is that you always have an option for an out. A part of me cannot wait to get to the Rainbow Valley and defeat this devil on my shoulder. The Rainbow Valley, when there is no option because there is no civilization around. Where I must find the strength to push through.

For now, however, there is an option. It's a house at the top of the next hill. And thank God this option exists. With the wind now at my back, I fly with the instability of my trailer shadowing me down the large hill. At the bottom I see a sign for an open market. I enter at the end of a small winding dirt driveway.

"Hello," I call to an elderly lady with short white hair and a great welcoming smile. I can instantly sense that she is down to earth. Maybe it's all the time she spends in the earth, or maybe it's just her Kiwi character. Either way it is obvious that she is the owner of this land.

"What can I do you for, dear?"

"Well, I am trying to get to Hanmer Springs."

"Well, you're a ways off. When do you want to get there by?" Her voice has a soft and calming tone.

"Tonight was the plan."

She looks up to see the sun beginning to make its way down to the horizon. It must be close to 5 p.m. She looks at her watch and then at me. Her blue eyes twinkle with amusement.

"Actually," I say, trying to draw the conversation away from my weakening attempt to reach Hanmer Springs, "I was wondering if you know of a post office nearby. I believe my trailer is too heavy and I cannot continue on with this weight."

"Chances be that the post office is right around the corner. The lady who runs it is named Debbie, and she will fix you up with whatever you may need. It is Easter Weekend, though, so I'm not sure if she's there."

"Thank you so much," I reply with panting breath as my bike wheels start to turn. Away I go, post office-bound. Right around the corner in a car is very different than right around the corner on a bike.

Unfortunately, Debbie is not at the post office when I arrive; however, her comrade tells me that she will be there in the morning. An inn across the street will serve as my perfect rejuvenation spot for the evening. I ride into the small parking lot, nestled in the foothills on Te Waipounamu (South Island), between Christchurch and my first day's failed destination of Hanmer Springs.

I struggle to position my trailer in a way that will allow my bike to lean effortlessly against the red-brown brick side of the inn. As I wrestle with my nemesis (known as the trailer), I feel gratitude for having the benefits of civilization. Without this post office, I would be screwed.

An English woman runs this quaint inn, and it seems to be a family establishment. "Sit down and have some food, lass," she says. I am inclined to say no, as I have much to figure out before tomorrow's ride, but her insisting motherly tone is too convincing. I take a seat at the maple bar, and she hands me a menu. Standard bar dishes fill the laminated page: meat pies, fish 'n' chips, lamb— an abundance of Kiwi fare.
I order some fresh salad, along with a main course of fish 'n' chips before heading upstairs to a small Victorian-style room with a warm, creaky bed. Right as my head hits the soft, inviting pillow...

41

ring, ring. I look over to see a cream-colored, 1950s-style phone centered on the nightstand.

"Hello?"

The thick English accent resounds in my ear.

"Sorry to bother, lass, but you have a phone call." *A phone call,* I think. *Who the heck knows I am here? Who the heck would call me?*

A man's voice comes over the phone. "Hey there, this is Richard."

"Richard who?" I am baffled.

"Richard from the farm down the road," he replies, as if I am supposed to know who he is. "You stopped by here earlier and mentioned to my wife that you're heading to Hanmer Springs. Well, she figures it's your route to get to Picton, and I wanted to warn you that the Rainbow Valley is closing in two days. Once those gates are closed, there's no getting through. Even if you take the Molesworth Muster Trail, it'll take you a good three nights to get through. The valley will be shut by then for Anzac Day."

For those who don't know their NZ history, Anzac Day is a national day of remembrance that broadly commemorates all Australians and New Zealanders who served and died in all wars, conflicts, and peacekeeping operations, and the contribution and suffering of all those who have served. Yes, that was taken straight from Wikipedia.

Shut for Anzac Day? You have got to be kidding me, I think. Anzac, Easter weekend, so many holidays, yet for some reason I don't remember getting these breaks from school.

"Okay, what do you suggest I do?" My mind is still trying to understand this whole conversation.

"I suggest you take the bus from here to Picton."

No way in hell am I taking a bus! That would be admitting defeat. I'm not even two days into cycling.

"How is the bus traveling? Can't I simply take the road the bus is taking over the mountains?"

"That's not allowed, it's incredibly dangerous and you'll get yourself run over. Don't be stubborn now. I know you want to bike but it's just not going to happen with the valley shutting down and the main highway up the coast closed."

I can tell by the tone of his voice that the comforts of his farm life had subdued his adventurous spirit. There is no point in continuing the conversation. I politely thank him for his sincere concern and hang up the phone. I mean, really, closing an entire valley? How bad could it be?

Before my mind has time to worry on the closing of Rainbow Valley, my head hits the pillow. This is my rest, my relaxation before beginning the task of sorting my gear.

The following morning commences with determining what is really necessary and what is simply luxury.

Two pairs of underwear = Luxury

One pair = Necessity

Now before you start thinking it's grossly unhygienic, take a moment to listen to my rationale: you don't wear underwear with biker shorts, so the only time I'll be wearing the underwear is while I'm in town. Besides, 1 pair + 2 sides = 4 pairs. Now that's some solid dirt-bag logic! I also brought two pairs of leggings for the city. Two is luxury; one of them must go. Two piles start to emerge of things that are necessity and things that are luxury. I have to be cutthroat, which comes far easier now that I have felt the weight of my excess baggage. Literally felt the weight.

My luxury pile is definitely taller than my necessity pile, which should tell me plenty. Although I love my darling trailer, it is obvious that the amount of things I am left with can be bungee-corded onto the bike racks, thus saving me the extra weight of a trailer. Life lessons.

With weight, always adhere to the Sierra Alpinist approach: light is always right. I thought I was light before, but I wasn't even close, and every tiny little bit of weight makes a difference when you're cycling up the hill, or even more so when you're in wind. Those two extra battery packs to make sure your phone is charged make you really pay attention to how much battery you are using on your phone. The other thing to go is my deodorant. I know it sounds a little bit uncivilized, but there is no way stench from my smelly pits would make up for the weight of a heavy deodorant stick. Following the tough deodorant decisions, I notice that for some reason I have two pairs of shoes. Also not necessary.

Final Count for Necessities:
- Pair of underwear
- Cycling shorts (currently wearing)
- Sports bra (currently wearing)
- Cycling top (currently wearing)
- Pair of socks (currently wearing)
- Individual leg pullovers, to cover my legs on a cold morning (currently wearing)
- Mid-layer fleece top
- Macpac lightweight rain pants
- Macpac lightweight rain jacket
- Macpac active leggings (city wear)
- Lightweight Nike tennis shoes
- Beanie
- Leave No Trace bag (to shit in when I don't have access to a dunny)
- Tent (two person, three-season)
- Sleeping bag
- Sleeping pad
- Cell phone
- Goal Zero solar power battery charger
- Lighter
- Spork (spoon+fork in one utensil = very fancy)
- Sea to Summit pot/bowl

- Pocket Rocket stove
- Gas canister
- 4 freeze-dried meals
- 15-inch GoPro
- Cash/card
- Passport (for identification, in case someone finds me frozen to my bike in the outback)
- MacBook Pro in its case

…My sanity!

Chapter Seven

The Fascination with Fabio

My alarm goes off at 7 a.m. The post office doesn't open until 10, so this will give me plenty of time to eat breakfast, stretch for the day's ride, and most importantly finalize sorting my gear. The pile of luxury items will be shipped on to Auckland, awaiting my arrival in 27 days' time. My necessities will need to be strapped to my bike—with bungee cord. I get this from the gas station across the street. The strapping process is not easy, requiring careful and precise placement of each item to prevent destruction of my necessities. Adjusting and packing tactics require constant realignment in order to make sure that all is secure on the back and front of my bike, evenly. I cannot afford to lose anything on this trip, especially since I am now stripped down to the basic of basics. Every last piece has to be fixed. If something comes off my bike, who knows how far back it would be and how much time I will waste cycling back to pick it up. Or worse, losing it forever.

When I think my bike is strapped to the best of my ability, I set it in the closed dining room of the inn. Then I carry my duffle bag of luxuries to the post office across the street to be mailed to Auckland.

"I think I saw you biking yesterday." Debbie, the

post office lady, tells me. "Passed you in my car. That was an awfully big trailer you had there. I was sure glad when Richard mentioned you would be coming in this morning."

"Richard?" I'm a little confused.

"Yes, Richard and his wife run the farm up the road, where you stopped yesterday."

I cannot help but laugh. Right when I begin to forget how small New Zealand is, suddenly I am reminded. *Oh fudge,* a thought enters my mind, *if I did hitch a ride, everyone in the country would know I cheated by the time I got to Auckland. I might actually have to finish this darn thing I started.*

I say a tearful goodbye to my bag of luxury and head back to the inn to grab my bike. 'Please exit out the back door', a handwritten note on the counter reads. Dressed to the nines in my cyclist getup, I gather my newly light bike. As I am trying to push the back door, it suddenly swings open to reveal a handsome mid-20s Kiwi farm hunk. He smiles at me and releases the door handle once I have successfully cleared the exit point. Without a word he turns to pick up an axe from its solid placement in a stump by the door.

"Thank you," I say, moving my bike away from the door. He winks at me and continues chopping wood for the fire, a task he had evidently been working on all morning. I rest my bike against his pile of wood and head back into the inn to retrieve the now-empty trailer.

"What are you going to do with that trailer?" the young handsome man asks upon my re-exit, as he wipes sweat from his brow. If this were a romance novel, he would be my Fabio (isn't that the guy's name who is on the cover of all the romance novels?). His dark-brown hair, tan skin, bushy black eyebrows and hazel eyes – there is just something about a farm boy. The definition of hard masculine labor.

"As you can see it is not attached to my bike, so I don't know," I reply, slightly smitten.

"Why do you have it?"

"I used it to get my luxuries from Christchurch to here, but it was way too heavy. I can't continue on with it."

"Luxuries?" He looks puzzled. He obviously doesn't get my sense of humor. But I will let this slide due to his Fabio-esque physique.

"Long story. Would you know of a recycling place?"

He thinks for a moment before replying. "No, but I will take it. I could turn it into something for the farm."

"Excellent. It's all yours," I say with a breath of relief.
He takes the metal end of the trailer from me. Our hands touch for a split second before I pull away. I re-center my concentration toward my bike, then begin to walk it onto the gravel

driveway that leads back to the paved motorway.

"Where are you going, anyway?"

I hop on my bike and smile back at him. "Auckland."

"Auckland?" he shouts after me. "Are you out of your mind?"

But I am already gone.

Chapter Eight
Steamy Goodness & Questionable Togs

The wind is not as strong as yesterday, and the hills do not seem quite as steep. In reality the hills' steepness has increased and the wind gusts are heavier than those of the previous day, but lightening my load eases the strain on my legs.

I must look insane while biking, for I have slid into the habit of saying a friendly hello to the many sheep and cows that graze the pastures along the motorway. Of course, it would be rude not to at least attempt their language, since I am technically a tourist in these parts. Every few kilometers a loud "mooooooo" or an over-dramatic "baaah-hhh" will be expelled from my throat. The animals' heads turn, ears perk, and funny facial gestures ensue. It is as if the cows are thinking, *What's wrong with this wild lady?*

I seem to be finding amusement in the simplest of activities.

With 70 kilometers of the day's ride behind me, the sun is starting to set. A feeling of accomplishment overcomes me. "Welcome to Hanmer Springs" the sign reads. I may be a full day behind schedule, but at this point I am just happy I even reached the springs.

I find an ideal campground situated just down the

road from the hot springs. It's not simply a place where campers and wanderers alike pitch for their night's rest, but also where over-zealous materialists park their RVs equipped with a queen bed, carpeted floor, and televisions for the "true camping experience". I check in with the main office attendant, pay my camper's fee, and get assigned a numbered site to pitch my tent.

Rolling my bike through the campground, I notice families cooking on the BBQ pits, children playing ball, and outdoor entertainment systems set up to watch the rugby game. Campgrounds have never been my first choice when on a nomadic adventure, but in the depths of a tourist town like this one, there is not much of a choice. I pitch my brand new two-person Macpac tent and set it up like a cozy home inside. Just before I begin to get too involved with my nesting, the mildly sulphur smell from the hot springs seeps past my tent flap, calling my name. Thank goodness for my campsite placement. Since last night my legs have had that ever-familiar ache of being overworked. Hot springs are the ideal solution before I enter into the "closed" Rainbow Valley. This way if I get lost in the valley, at least I will have relaxed muscles while I starve to death.

Hot spring heaven awaits.

My problem is now I am light on gear, the only thing I have are the cycling shorts I am wearing and my leggings. Although it would be a fashion statement to swim in my cycle shorts, I cannot afford to get them (either of them) wet. My muscle pain increasing by the second, I waddle across the street to the hot springs entrance and to my delight, surprise, and a little bit of disgust, I read that they have togs for rent.

"One, please, and a pair of togs," I say to the skinny ginger-haired kid in his late teens. He hands me a black Speedo. Life is just too short not to take every single opportunity to soak in hot springs.

One of my favorite things about travelling alone is it opens up opportunities for conversation that you might not otherwise have. I find that when I travel with someone, my thoughts and my focus are melding around them, and vice versa. But when alone, I am open to constant communication opportunities, to learn more about life, the environment, and other people's worlds. Being a firm believer that everyone in life should do at least one trip alone, I don't preach about opportunities because I am sitting in a hot pool all by my lonesome; I preach this for the simple reason that some of the most important encounters in my life have occurred because I was alone on an adventure. Don't get me wrong, there are moments where I feel lonely, but in that loneliness I grow to appreciate the people who are in my life, the people I would want on the trip with me. In the solitude of my solo experience, I can be at one with my own thoughts. At least I should be at one with my own thoughts when I reach the Rainbow Trail.

Sitting in the hot springs I'm surrounded by tourists. More than anything, I had an idealistic view of returning to New Zealand. When I left here 10 years ago, there were not as many travelers from faraway lands discussing their recent tour of *The Lord of the Rings* set in almost-incomprehensible, broken English. Perhaps I simply grew up in an area where not as many tourists passed through like they do here in Hanmer Springs.

A little anxiety creeps into my thoughts about the coming days, not just because I am passing through the Rainbow Trail, which is known to be incredibly difficult, but also because I have arranged a meeting with Graeme. *Who is Graeme?* you might ask. Brace yourself, for I am about to get a little emotional.

After my father and brother passed away, memorial services were held around the world (partly because we moved around so much the friendship base was spread out, partly because my dad was a little bit famous, and mostly because it was such a tragedy that touched so many lives). The main memorial service for my father was held here in New Zealand. There were multiple people facilitating this service and for reasons I won't take time to explain, I was banned from attending my father's memorial. The person who banned me was Graeme. Almost four years after I had called to ask where the service would be held and was sternly told I was not welcome to attend, I decided for the sake of being the better person in life, now I had returned to New Zealand, that I would give him a call. The phone call happened just after my summit of Mt. Aspiring and before my arrival in Christchurch. I figured I would have today's cycle to Hanmer Springs and the next few days alone in the Valley to strategize how my encounter with Graeme might go.

The conversation was a little bit awkward, and I'm not quite sure that he understood how incredibly upset I was with him. He invited me to come by his house, which happens to be on the way between the Rainbow Trail and my next destination. It's in the town of Blenheim, known for its wine, and will serve as my last stop before reaching Picton, where I will take the ferry over to Wellington—provided I am not arrested for the murder of the aforementioned Graeme. My temper tends to get a grip on me sometimes, and the banning from my own father's memorial has been festering for the last four years.

Perhaps I shouldn't go, I tell myself. In my recent years of meditation and self-discovery I have consciously made an effort to make the right choices in potentially detrimental situations. Every part of my mind was screaming at me to not go by the home of Graeme Giles. *There's no point, it's done. You don't need anything from him. Just leave it alone and walk away.* Was it my angel or my devil telling me this? How do I know the right thing to do in this situation? *I am an adult now, not the bratty pre-teen that Graeme and many of my father's friends remember me as. I am an adult now.* Perhaps if I tell myself this enough times, I will start to believe it. I will start to believe that I am a mature woman who knows how to elegantly handle a situation that makes me want to explode.

The mists over the hot springs take my mind back to our conversation four years ago. It's a conversation that I will never forget, someone telling me that I can't say goodbye to my own father. It was hard enough I didn't have the bodies of my father or my brother. Bad enough that they would forever lie in the mountain of K2.

I was able to find comfort in saying goodbye to my brother, surrounded by his friends in California, but the Christchurch memorial service was my chance to say goodbye to my father. My father whom I loved more than anything as a little girl, my father whom I butted heads with as a pre-teen, my father whom I infuriated and left as a teenager. My father who desperately wanted my attention for the last six years of his life, my father whom I was so angry with, so hurt by. My father whom I wanted nothing to do with, I even went so far as to change my last name because I believed that he didn't have the right to carry the same name as me. He wasn't worthy of the title of "father". I told him this. In fact, not only did I tell him that, those were some of my last words to him.

Four years ago I was so broken, so desperate to be able to tell my father that I didn't mean what I said and that I loved him. Although there was no body for me to say this to, for some reason I believed that attending the Christchurch memorial service for Marty Schmidt was my chance to say those words to him. To say goodbye in a way that a daughter should be able to say goodbye to her father, to tell him that the only reason I hated him so much was because I loved him so much. To tell him that I was sorry. To tell him. To tell him. To tell him.

56

I can taste a salty tear falling down my check, fusing with the salty water surrounding my body. I look down at my fingers, like dripping raisins, and wonder if that conversation four years ago is what spurred this eternal search. It occurs to me that it doesn't matter what ignited it. It was lit and I am glad it was. This search is something more than just a search; it is an adventure. The more I adventure, the more I seem to learn about this world and, most of all, about myself: my life's purpose, my time here on this earth, my journey to grow my soul. As I curl into my sleeping bag, my mind comes back to the present as my eyes leave the level plane.

Chapter Nine

Farewell to Civilization

The first rays of morning light filter through my tent wall as if it were mosaic glass on a historic church in the depths of Europe. This is one of the joys of spending time in Mother Nature—you are not just on the world, but you're really in it. My body is slowly re-learning how to tell the time in the morning without looking at a clock, but rather by seeing the simple rays of light. In my previous adventures it has taken a few days to adjust to the nomadic way of life. First morning in the tent and I am already adjusting. Perhaps my Mt. Aspiring climb helped add a little dirt to my bag.

The smell of fresh dew on the ground is bracing, and I have a picturesque view from the vantage point of my now-unzipped tent. My eyes fixate on a single blade of lush green grass, a tiny ball of water perched on its tip.

Come on, Sequoia, wake up. The sleeping bag is warm and cozy. The last thing I want to do right now is expose my sore muscles to the chill of the morning and pack my stuff to be ready for the Rainbow Trail.

Rumors are that the first 500 meters of the trail are brutal. As overdramatically eloquent as that word may be, it is the correct description. As the paved road beneath my feet comes to an end, so does my excitement for the day's adventure. The incline is just ahead of me and boy oh boy, does it look brutal.

These first 500 meters are called Jacks Pass, which is the only way into this side of the Rainbow Trail. I was forewarned about the steepness of today's escapade up the pass. The long, treacherous, winding hill awaits me. It is gravel, not paved road, still accessible to cars but a truck would be recommended to take on the task of Jacks or the Rainbow Trail.

My tires skid out from the dusty rocks that make up this pass of Jacks. Every inch of my back and body is pushing forward, screaming at me, but my mind stays strong. I can feel my back tires begin to lift off the gravel to the harsh sounds of continuous skids. My balance is unsteady, and each circular motion my feet take is countered by a swift jolt as my tires skid beneath me. Suddenly my front wheel veers right, completely out of my control. I attempt to counter with my arms but it's too late. My bike skids against the gravel and I hurl to the ground.

My body is sure going to feel that one in the morning. To add insult to injury, a man in a pickup pulls up next to me.

"Are you okay, lass?"

"Yes, I'm fine, thanks," I say, slightly embarrassed.
Flashbacks of my training on Venice Beach's paved roads are rushing through my mind.

I have been told by a few passersby that this is one of the most difficult sections of the Rainbow, and it definitely shows. However, the fact that Jacks Pass seems to be my challenge for the day keeps me strong, for I know if I can make it up and over this harsh terrain, a downhill awaits.

Unfortunately, my bike tires (26x1.5-inch Maxxis Gypsy) on my Surly hybrid, along with the gears on my cycle, will not allow me to ride up this steep gravel road. Instead, my concentration is aimed at walking/pushing my bike up. Moaning and groaning in synchronicity to my uphill grind, I lick my lips. The taste of salty sweat seems most prominent. If you were to extract my audio right now, it would sound like I was giving birth to a baby elephant.

A family on mountain bikes passes by, peddling along. "Put it in a lower gear," the brother yells back at his sister, who is almost in full tears as she tries her hardest to stay on her bike.

"Come on, Sarah," the mother calls back. The father hops off his bike and runs down to help his daughter, holding her bike by the seat and handlebars. He helps guide her along. He is holding her steady as they continue up the hill. They are parallel with me now and they both look over at me as I huff and puff, pushing my bike.

"You want to trade bikes with her?" the dad asks Sarah.

We all giggle.

"You're doing amazing, stay strong," I say as they pass me. Words of encouragement always seem to help. In this moment I could use some serious words of encouragement. Surprisingly, my phone has reception.

On a trip like this, a trip that has sponsors and people at home interested in my progress, there is an underlying understanding that social media should be happening throughout this ride. So to inform the public and gain some words of encouragement, I jump on Facebook Live. I turn the camera down the steep hill and show my friends and minimal interested onlookers what they are missing. My life is not all fun adventures... well, most of it seems to be lately, but it is also pushing bikes up hills and wanting nothing more than a pickup truck and maybe a massage at the top. I titled the post *Cycling around NZ*, and one of the first comments from some random was "You are going from Christchurch to Auckland... that's not around NZ, damn Americans." Just the kind of encouragement I was looking for!

Darn social media, it gives everyone a platform for voicing their opinions. The fact is, some people just don't deserve to have a platform. There, I said it. Some people are just too damn ignorant to have the right to voice their opinion publically. So, given that I pride myself on not letting my temper get the best of me when it comes to stupidity in the age of social media, I will save my counter-argumentative venting for precious pages in this book. Valuable real estate.

I. First of all, he may be correct in that I'm not actually cycling *around* NZ; however, in my humble opinion, cycling across 3/4 of the country sure as heck counts, or at least I think it does right now as I'm pushing my bike up this God-forsaken hill. And anyone who wishes to protest my cycling length, until you are on a bike riding beside me, I don't want to hear a gobsmackle of what you have to say.

II. Secondly, although I am an American citizen and currently live there—I can assure you that I am just as much Kiwi as the next *pākehā* girl. I was born in Aotearoa (New Zealand). This is the land of my birth and I have dual passports to prove it. I was officially adopted by Ngāti Kahungunu iwi and carry the middle name of Karanema. I grew up for the first part of my life in this powerful land and will forever have it as my home.

III. Thirdly, negative social media commenters can kiss my sweet gluteus maximus (which will be nice and firm by the time this ride has wrapped).

Needless to say my Facebooking for encouragement didn't exactly pan out as well as I hoped. But alas, social media never seems to.

My phone starts to buzz. I still have service. Fantastic! I look at my buzzing connection to civilization to see it is one of my closest friends, La-Ra, an Aussie who is working in film and living in NYC. She is one of my fascinatingly sophisticated friends who can always pull off a

62

single-wrap scarf. Let me tell you, it's not easy to pull off a single-wrap scarf.

"You okay, darling?" her tone indicates she must have been watching the live feed.

"This is not fucking easy, Ra."

"Well, it never was going to be a walk in the park," she reminds me.

"I changed my mind. I'll take the walk in the park."

She bursts out in laughter. "You will be so proud of yourself when you finish this." La-Ra is always full of encouragement.

When undertaking large adventures, it is always important to have a few close friends who can call you to remind you of who you are and why you are doing this.

"You got this," she says with strength in her voice. There it is, that's what I needed to hear. Even though it's something I already knew—it's something I needed to hear, from a friend's mouth to my ears! With my courage mustered, I power on.

A little way up the hill I see a jolly-looking man in a red shirt biking toward me. He slows to a stop and says, "Hi, I'm Grumm." The words run boisterously out of his large over-excited mouth.

"Hi, Grumm, I am Sequoia," I reply, catching his

contagious excitement.

"Are you taking the Rainbow?"

"Yes, planning to."

"I just dropped a girl up there named Jo. I am a cyclist myself. Been around the world for the last two years."

"Wow." I am instantly impressed by his slight insanity.

"That's why I hosted Jo and other cyclists. I'm a member of Warm Showers."

The warm showers Grumm is referring to is not the sexual innuendo that your dirty mind may think, but rather an app/website that allows cyclists to get a warm shower, bed, and a meal from hosts. I have been hearing all about it on this trip and plan to download the app when I get to Wellington and put it to good use.

"Jo has a lot more stuff than you. We had to cut down half of her belongings but she still far outweighs you."

"I had a lot more stuff, too. I packed up half of it and shipped it to meet me in Auckland. This is all I have left."

Eyeing my bungee cords and minimalist packaging that could easily be misconstrued as ghetto, Grumm sniggers. "Well, make sure you pick up some panniers when you get to your next

64

town—probably Blenheim."

"That's the plan," I say with a smile.

Grumm mounts his bike. "Happy riding," he says, beaming, and like that he's off.

The top of Jacks Pass is now in sight. A grin beams across my face. For some reason, whenever I see the finish line, the summit of a peak, or the end of any kind, no matter how tired I am I always conjure up a last burst of energy to end on a bang. I ran cross-country throughout school, and every race I would burn myself to the end of my wick and be running on fumes until I saw the finish line. Upon visibility of the end point, something would overtake me and I would muster the energy to cross it in a heroic sprint.

This last section of Jacks Pass feels like the finish line of a cross-country race. Full force ahead until I proudly reach the top of the pass, taking in a deep breath as my feet touch the flat ground. Turning around, the sky is cloudless, naked, an elegant baby blue in perfect contrast with the vibrant green valley far below. Recent rains in this area caused a brightening of the greenery, bringing fresh life to the earth, almost as if the valley floor were painted.

"The Rainbow Trail is really bumpy," a voice from behind me says. I turn around to see an older, tall women staring at my bike, which leaned against a post by the sign for the trails. She looks as if she has ridden around the world a few times herself. Her leg muscles put mine to shame and her smile lines are as deep as the Rainbow Valley. Pure grit. An inspiration.

"It is?" I respond, my naïveté shining through.

They say that part of experiencing adventures like this is learning as you go. Well, so far, it seems like I know nothing about what I am doing—so I guess I'm definitely "experiencing". I cannot help the sense of being completely knowledge-less on this trip. I have my maps, and my Google results for "biking across NZ", but none of that seems to make a difference until you are in the thick of it! Learning from people like Grumm about panniers (bags that attach to your bike so you don't have to use bungee cords).

"Your name isn't Jo, is it?"

"You just missed her – she's carrying a heavy load, that one," the gritty woman replies.

"I wonder if I will catch her in the Valley."

She eyes my bungee cords with judgment.
"Without panniers, your stuff is going to have a hard time staying on. The bumps will knock it right off."

With the realization that there is nothing I can do about that now, I thank her for her words of wisdom and head along the remaining flat section forming the top of Jacks Pass. My tires skid to a halt as I reach the edge of what looks like the winding downhill road that leads to the entrance of my presumed demise. I pull on the bungee cord just to test it is secure. Like an elastic band, I hear it snap back to its pre-set position.

The gritty woman was right. Within the first 100 meters I notice my tightly secured belongings on the front of my bike are beginning to wobble like a Jamaican girl's booty. If my front is a visible sign of the insecurity of my possessions, I can only imagine what is going on with the stuff behind me. The wind is strong, and holding my handlebars is no easy feat. The road's acne is thrusting me in every direction. It's too hard to turn my body to get a glance at my backside.

On the back of my bike, two bungees secure the majority of my necessities, including but not limited to my tent, sleeping bag, stove. All items I cannot afford to lose. Especially now that I am approaching the middle of nowhere, a far cry from civilization. I keep my focus and simply pray that I am not scattering stuff down this winding hill.

Alas, my brownie points with the big guy upstairs must be at an all-time low—for my prayers are not answered. Not only are they not answered, my peripheral vision can make out items flying left and right off my bike. I slam on my brakes. Skiiiddddd…. Thump.

And just like that I am in one piece with my bike. Slammed on my side, bike lying on top of me, feet still clipped it. This one is going to hurt in the morning, I can already tell. I twist my ankles and unclip. Circling the road to collect my belonging, my diagnosis of the issue presents itself. First and foremost is the matter of the bungee cords. My equipment must be secured tighter. But secondly is my crash. Because I slammed on my brakes, I did not allow enough time to unclip before becoming one with the hard earth. Because the ground consists primarily of gravel, and because my tires are hybrid and not straight mountain bike tires...... well, this is going to be a long-ass valley.

I re-mount my belongings, being extra cautious with the bungee, and double and triple checking my strap-abilities. I walk my bike until reaching a less bumpy section of the jarring road. Once there is a little more consistency in the gravel level, I hop back on.

Within a kilometer, the God-forsaken gyrating commences again. It is a slight downhill, and the indents in the gravel seem to worsen. This time is far more frustrating than before. I open my mouth and let out a solid hum. But because of the bumps, my solid hum becomes a confused melody. A muddle of odd noises is caused by the movement in my body. However, these noises can act as my gauge for the upcoming road of frustration. I can use the movement in my vocal cords to judge the severity of the bumps and maybe allow me to guestimate at what point my belongings will tumble. This tactic will save me a little time of having to walk back up the hill to collect items after my crash. But for right now, on this hill... thoughts and prayers for my belongings... thoughts and prayers.

My prayers are being blatantly ignored. I hear the sounds of items falling off my bike. I can just make out the falling objects between the gyrations of my bike's tires against the gravel. My hand reaches for my back brakes and I slowly pull the lever toward me, knowing that if I pull the brakes too hard I will skid out of control again.

But as my bike begins to come to a halt—it is moving too slowly and the wheels are getting caught in the now-thick gravel—I cannot unclip. My wheels are moving uncontrollably. "FUCKKKK!" I scream out as the bike falls on top of me. This time leaving a large gash on my leg. I can feel the open wound before I see it, and it doesn't feel very good. I lie for a second in my frustration. Take a deep breath and then look down. Gravel is lodged in my flesh, pieces of skin hanging.

I scramble for my first aid kit—which is tucked deep in my sleeping bag case—one of the necessities that fell off and is now 20 meters back. Sliding myself out from under my bike, I hobble to gather my belongings. How pitiful I must look. No more than 10 kilometers into the valley, I have already fallen twice, lost my belongings, and scraped my leg.

I bite my lip and let out a moan as I use tweezers to remove the lodged gravel and excess skin fragments, followed by a small screech as I apply an alcohol swab to the open skin. The last thing I need is to be stuck in the middle of nowhere with an oozing infection because I was too much of a pussy to apply alcohol. In my first aid kit is a single Ace wrap bandage. I apply some Neosporin and then wrap my leg. The temperature is starting to cool – and since I am already at a stand-still, I dig through my necessities and find my leg warmers. Think of a ballet dancer's leg warmers, except not nearly as feminine. Aesthetics lose their value in the valley. Practicality outweighs all other factors when in survival mode.

At this rate, the Rainbow Trail will take me three times as long as I thought, constantly having to stop and pick up my belongings as they fall from my gyrating bicycle.

Bike, lose equipment, fall, scream.
Bike, lose equipment, fall, scream.
Bike, lose equipment, fall, scream.

This cycle continues for the next seven hours. It reaches a point where I feel like crying, I am so emotionally drained and in physical pain. Why am I doing this to myself? My entire body is bruised – my legs are covered in scrapes and gouges – my spine is all kinds of out of alignment... and this is only the first day in the valley.

It's almost dark now and I have to squint to make out the trail ahead. I just need to make it to a point where I can see a flat section to camp. Ideally it would be before a section called Island Saddle, but because of my issues and the darkness coming in, I can barely tell where I am. In my first round of calculations, I was supposed to arrive at Island Saddle at approximately 3 p.m. It is now 6:30 p.m.!

I literally cannot see. This is incredibly dangerous. I hit the brakes, unclip, and walk to the left of the

70

road. The frontage is made up of grass that is slanted down—or perhaps the road I just came from is slanting up and the grass is flat. Or perhaps I am losing my mind. Either way there is a dirt mound leading from the road down to the grass. I lean my bike against it and grab my easily accessible headlamp.

First things first. A jacket. The temperature has definitely dropped to a chilly degree. Once a jacket is on, I undo the bungee cords and grab my tent. I had time to master the setup back at Hanmer Springs. After it's assembled, I unload everything inside – sleeping bag, stove, toiletries, and food. I huddle in my tent and begin boiling some water in the vestibule. Recognizing it will take a moment for the water to boil, I take out one of my necessities – Tiger Balm – and apply it to each bruise. Almost my whole body is covered in Tiger Balm.

For those who have never experienced the heavenly ointment that is Tiger Balm, you are in for a treat. However, the scent of the balm can make you a little drowsy. In my case, having my body lathered in it, it knocks me out.

A few forced bites of my cardboard-tasting, freeze-dried meal, a cup of hot cocoa, and my body is in the sleeping bag, my headlamp is turned out, and so am I.

Chapter Ten

Pedaling through Pain

I can see my breath. The condensation on the outside of my sleeping bag is beading up.

Morning time is the period of my day that seems to take the most self-motivation. I am forced into a circumstance of survival to self-motivate, like I might not have otherwise been accustomed to. This is one of my favorite parts about venturing into the wilderness, the discovery of my own abilities.

I rise and shine to the morning sun which acts as a dryer for my tent, which is still swimming in frost. Not only my tent, for as I exit my sleeping quarters I see that my bike, leaning against the nearby mound of dirt, is frozen stiff. The frame is covered in a thick layer of ice and so is the seat. So much so, that if I were to stick my bare ass on it I have a feeling it would not detach.

Picking up my bike, I place it directly in the sun's gleam, along with my tent. With the first rays of light, I see to my delight that I am positioned just under Island Saddle.

Island Saddle is the "hilly" section of the Rainbow Trail, much like Jacks Pass, only shorter (thank God). Distance seems irrelevant when you cannot see your end point.

I pack my now-dry belongings, arranging them in order on my bike. Meaning that the many hours spent losing and re-mounting my belongings allowed me to rearrange them. This resulted in establishing a precise and sequential order that permitted as tight a fit as bungee-able. With all the pain of yesterday's ride, I actually learned a system to implement for a more efficient journey... hopefully.

Island Saddle is steep and sweat-producing.
Grunting and moaning, I make my way up the winding gravel road, most of which I am having to walk, as the hill's steepness, along with my load, offers an impossible ride. My mind scrambles for motivation to keep pushing forward.

My brother would be proud of me, I think.

I have these vivid memories of when I thought I wasn't good enough in the eyes of my brother. I know that this was not the case—he was never a judgmental soul—this was simply a belief that I projected upon myself. However, since his passing, each time I do something I know that he would be proud of, whether it be hosting an event for the foundation I started in his name, reaching the summit of a tough climb, or in this case, making it to the top of Island Saddle, comes a feeling of pride, not just for my own efforts but for the fact that I know my brother would be proud.

It is a tough thing to have a great loss, to face the ongoing path of grief, for it is an ongoing path. At what point is your loved one's journey forgotten? What I mean by that is, my journey of self-discovery is constantly taking place through my grief. A concentration on my loss powers my personal experience. It does not control it, but it does motivate it.

Lately the concentration has been on becoming the best that I can be by trusting my own judgment. After my father and brother were killed, I spent a great amount of time concentrating on why they went up the mountain when everyone else went back. One of the climbers who was on K2 that year said, "It's because they were the strongest climbers on the mountain." I spent a while thinking about that answer. When you know yourself, and when you know your own abilities better than others do, why would you not trust your own instincts?

Adventurer Kyle Dempster once said (quoting the poet Robert Frost): "Two roads diverged, and I took the one less traveled." I repeat this aloud as the last part of my tough final push up the Saddle approaches.
I took the one less traveled.

My inspiration is drawn from Kyle's voice. Sadly, Kyle, like my father and brother, like Dean Potter, Hayden Kennedy, and so many other adventurous spirits, was taken from us too soon. There is something fiercely independent about adventurous spirits. I believe it comes with learning about who you really are as a person.

You learn this by putting yourself in physically and mentally challenging situations. You learn this by taking yourself out of your comfort zone, and as a result this provides an insight into who you are and what you are truly capable of.

Others' advice is just that, advice. Sometimes you need to find out for yourself what really lies on the path ahead. For example, between Christchurch to right now, trudging up Island Saddle, I had a total of seven people tell me, in some form or another, not to venture into Rainbow Valley:

> "Your tires are a little small for that kind of a road!"
> "Are you sure you want to go all alone?"
> "The gate will be locked and there is no way you will make it to the exit."
> "That is not the smartest idea."

If had listened to just one of those many opinion-givers, I would not be witnessing the beauty and sweat propulsion that the Rainbow Trail is currently providing me. Because I know my own abilities, because I know what my body and mind are capable of, I am willing to forge on ahead and leave the naysayers in the dust, if for nothing more than to find out for myself if my tires will not work, or if the gate will be locked.

In the case of my father and brother, I am beginning to understand why they felt the need to continue on, to find out the conditions for themselves, and not blindly trust the opinions of others.

When you take the road less traveled, when you forge your own path in this life, you are able to experience the smells and tastes this earth has to offer without barriers or boundaries. When you take the road less traveled, you are able to feel the height of human emotion and see sights unseen to the common eye. Your existence is not definable but rather transcended. Sometimes, there is sacrifice involved. Sometimes, taking the path less traveled results in death. The question is not whether you want to die, but rather how you want to live.

My ever-evolving life is now lived on top of a bike, on top of the Island Saddle, and it feels incredible. A rush of adrenaline shoots through me as my bike lines up to begin my descent. To my delight there are no bumps on this side of the Saddle. There are many potholes that require avoiding, but no gyrating bumps to toss my belongings from my home on wheels.

After you have spent an exhausting effort making it to the top of a tough hill, there is no greater feeling than to descend in free fly. Wind whips through my hair and I let out a howl, thankful to notice there is no movement in my vocal tone— no gyration in my bike —just smooth sailing. The length of descent, although satisfying, does not do justice to the physical exhaustion from the climb. The road begins to even out again. This time its length stretches into the distant hills, revealing no immediate climbs ahead. Lush greens mix with golden browns of the New Zealand landscape. You cannot paint this beauty; this is a beauty that must be witnessed, experienced. A tree of autumn rests in solitude on an abundance of lush green.

The sound of water is ever-present in the Rainbow Valley, from the rush of a large river to the trickle of a small stream. I look to my right and notice the water dancing beside me in the form of a flowing river. Resting my bike against the edge where the gravel meets the grass, I detach my knapsack of nourishment from my bike's back mount and take a seat by the stream. It is almost midday now, and, apart from the sounds of water and birds, my mind is as clear as the volume-less wind.

This morning's activity is proof of my evolving hypothesis that the more physically exhausted one becomes, the more relaxed one's mind is, and the more a possibility of enlightenment presents itself. Perhaps *enlightenment* isn't the word. I guess the best way to describe it would be a connection to "what is". Either what is present, or what is spiritual. What is, is all around us. And a relaxed mind is open to soak it in. With my toes in the bubbling stream, my fingers caressing the grassy bank, a deep breath of freshness in my lungs, I do not think I have ever, or will ever, experience this kind of relaxation again. A connection to What is.

Chapter Eleven

The Necessity of Deodorant

I stink. Like, seriously stink. You know you smell really bad when your own stench begins to feel normal in your nostrils. My sweat of the last few days, mixed with my unhygienic inability to change clothes because I pared down weight to carry a lighter load, has done me in.

Thank God I don't have any company on this trip. Perhaps I shall call this journey "stench in solitude". My dating prospects are getting slimmer by the second.

Most likely we are both fortunate I never did find Jo. She would have been off put by my unique reek. This elusive woman that Grumm described, with her over-loaded bike that most likely contained a change of clothes. I bet she was hygienic and didn't smell like a musky sewer.

I have to admit, I am beginning to question whether Jo actually exists. She seems to have made a fast run through the valley. I would imagine if she were carrying a load of belongings, she would not have been so speedy with her river wading.

For now, at this point in the Valley, I have begun the tedious task of river-wading. Sometimes, when I am lucky and my bike is fast and the river is simply a stream, I am able to ride through my road's impediment. It's not just water that would have slowed Jo's pace, but gates also. For the warnings of the "Closing of the Rainbow Trail" proved to be valid over the day's ride. So far, I have had to jump three locked gates. I did this by hoisting my bike over my head like Wonder Woman—it wasn't nearly as heroic as it sounds—and placing it on the other side before hopping the gate myself. To be frank, I came out of each gate debacle with a new bump or bruise to add to my already banged-up body.

The roads vibration is no longer an issue, but in reality a part of me preferred that obstacle in comparison to the locked gates and more: my current predicament concerning water.

Every few kilometers of what I hope and pray is the last section of the Rainbow Valley, a body of water presents itself across my path. Sometimes, it is simply a trickle, sometimes a larger stream, and now near the latest barricade—it is a massive river.

Dismounted from my bike, I gaze in awe of this miraculously fast-moving body of water. First, I must assess the abundant liquid for the best possible way to cross. Leaning my bike against a large rock on the bank of the rushing river, I stroll up and down, twiddling my thumbs until I see my access point. Unfortunately, I cannot tell the approximate depth of the river's mid-point. Either way, I will have to make two trips. One with my bike, and one with my belongings.

I strip down to my birthday suit (to not get my only pair of riding clothes wet). Placing my shoes and clothes in the large drawstring bag that currently holds some of my other necessities, I rest it next to my tent and other belongings that will be left on the river bank for the second load.

My toe touches the water and instantly my nipples become erect. *Holy fuck!* Profanity of the extreme reels through my mind. I take a deep breath, in through my nose and slowly, meditatively, release it through my mouth. *Come on, Sequoia. This is just water. Remember the rush that cold water gives you. You love that rush. You are addicted to that rush.* With that self-motivation, my confidence is as rigid as my nipples. Away I go. Strong and steady, my bike lifted above my naked body.

What a sight I must be, wading into waist-high current, my bicycle hoisted above my head. Stark naked. Heavily breathing. Pushing through the rapids. If only there was a camera to capture this monumental moment of agony.

Finally, I reach the other side without grace or ease, and rest my stripped bike against the river's opposing bank. The word *cold* does not even begin to describe this water. It sends electric chills through my body as I make my way back across to gather my remaining necessities. Surprisingly, it is far more difficult to cross with nothing hoisted on my shoulders. I guess there is no weight added to my body to allow me to be more sturdy in the whisking rapids. Thus, necessity-less I have to fight to stay on a straight path. My eyes fixated on the pile of my belongings nestled among the rocks.

After I have successfully made it back across, hoisted my necessities on my shoulders, and crossed the roaring river once more, I begin the tedious task of getting dressed. For a tedious task, it is. Trying to pull spandex over wet skin is like trying to get foreigners not to pre-judge you when an American accent rolls off your tongue.

At least my recent soak will help diminish my body odor.

Just as my shirt is being pulled over my still-wet torso, I hear the rev of a motorbike in the not too distant future. The engine's hum remains present as I lift my cycle and start reattaching my belongings. By the time my bike's bungee'd up in a neat package, the hum presents itself. A dirt bike appears, followed quickly by a second. Their engines now a full roar, and they are coming straight for me. In a haze of dust, the two bikers skid within a few meters of my upright cycle. Because that is sooooo attractive. Rev your engine and cover a girl in dirt, That's how to get a lady's attention (insert eye roll here).

The engines turn off. The peace and quiet of nature returns.

"Hey ya," one rider's voice becomes unmuffled as he takes off his helmet to reveal a face only a mother could love.

"Hi," I reply out of politeness.

The other biker's helmet is off now. Chunky cheeks to match his heavy-set exterior. He was probably handsome once, in his late teens and early twenties. The kind of guy who could pull a few chicks in his day, but had let too many brews and barbeque feasts settle in his stomach.

"Beautiful day for a ride," the mother-loved man says. They are both big men. In different ways, but big enough to know I wouldn't want them getting any ideas or I would be in a little trouble. He eyes my bike.

"Well, I wouldn't want to be riding that, though. That looks like lot of work." He sniggers with a glance to his partner in crime. "You haven't done the whole trail, have ya?"

"I have."

"Well, not yet, still got a little ways to go." He pauses and looks me up and down in a way that makes my stomach turn. "It's impressive, though. You must be really fit to bike something like this." I can sense a shift in the air. "I bet you've got a tight body on you." The hairs on the back of my neck stick straight up. He hasn't wasted any time to become incredibly creepy.

"You must have trained hard for this ride," Chunky Cheeks cuts in.

"Sure did. But I'm a black belt in jujitsu, so it keeps me in shape," I say in a sharp and confident tone. I have never done a single lesson in jujitsu—but they don't need to know that.

"Woooo, watch out for fighter girl." The ugly one laughs. And then locks his eyes on me. An unnerving smirk pasted to his pale face. "Out here all alone, are ya?"

My mind scrambles for a reply.

"A girl would be stupid to do this trail alone. My boyfriend's waiting up the road."

"Really?" says Chunky. "We didn't see nobody."

"He's probably setting up camp." *Fuck. I shouldn't have let them know I was camping.*

"We're camping out, too," Chunky replies. "You're welcome to hang with us. Have a brew, or two." He winks. I feel vomit in the back of my throat.

"Thanks, but I should be going." I pick up my helmet from the ground.

"I would give you my number," the ugly man smirks, "but there's no reception anywhere round these parts."

I get the feeling he's trying to tell me something. Something I already know.
I already know that my phone doesn't work.
I already know that he knows there is no boyfriend.

I already know that it's just me and these two idiots, alone in this valley.

I already know... that if I scream, no one can hear me.

"Good thing I have a Sat phone," I say, flashing a bold smile while mounting my bike.

I don't have a Sat phone. Well, I did, at one point back in Waipara, but it was tossed in the "Luxury" pile back when I had to decide whether to take the extra weight in a Sat phone...or in food. At this moment, I think I would rather starve.

"Enjoy the day," I say, and begin riding toward what looks like a forest.

Chapter Twelve

Not a Pot of Gold in Sight

The Rainbow's end is in the near distance; I can feel it. The ever-accountable morning light touches the corner of my tent, and the drops from last night's rain lie dormant on the fabric that makes up the roof of my erect dwelling. I did not sleep much last night. Between the sounds of the wildlife and the two dirt bikers lingering in the valley, my nerves would allow me only a moment or two of drifting off. The dawn could not arrive too soon. With the first hint of light hitting my tent, I awake and pack my sleeping bag. Only around 30 kilometers more and I should reach Highway 63 which, if I simply follow the motorway, will lead me straight to Blenheim.

Stuffing my tent poles into their bag, I begin the morning task of assembling my belongings in their sequential order, to rest atop the front and back racks of my bike. Bungee attached. Bike mounted. Feet clipped. Away I go. To my delight and joy, within five kilometers my trail dissolves into a paved road. Civilization is beginning to emerge.

One thing that has remained consistent is the hilly landscapes. However, paved hills are a joy in comparison.

As I reach the top of my first paved hill. I cannot

help but beam with pride. I am capable of more than I thought. I am capable of staying strong to my goal, not allowing my physical or emotional hits to deter me from my path. What a remarkable feeling this is. To overcome my own fears. My own doubts. To stand atop a paved road after three long days of human-less (minus two creeps) contact and emotional bullets. My moment of reflection has given me my morning burst of energy that will take me through today's long ride. I take a deep breath and push off from the pavement.

My tires move faster and faster, propelling my bike and body. My hands release from the handlebars—smiling from ear to ear, I open my mouth to the sound of my own voice echoing in the wind.

"Ask me again why I'm doing this... it's for this moment right here, this moment right here— wind in my hair, no other human beings in sight.... It's FREEEDOMMMM!"

I let out a howl which soars with the wind and concludes with a genuinely happy laugh. The height of human emotion. For what is our purpose on this earth, if not to experience every human emotion possible?

Upon my arrival to the end of the Rainbow Valley, the road leads to an abrupt T of Highway 63. It's busy, very busy for a New Zealand road. I would imagine the large truck and abundance of traffic whizzing by are all due to the detour of the road from the recent earthquake. The Kaikoura earthquake that occurred at 12:02 a.m. on November 14, 2016, was a whopping 7.8 magnitude. The earthquake killed two people and also killed the Kaikoura coastline, its railway lines, and Highway 1, which serves as the main road from Christchurch to Picton/Blenheim. As a result, all traffic was re-routed through Highway 63, a smaller and windier mountain motorway.

Six more hours of dodging trucks, self-encouragement, and talking to sheep. There are plenty of sheep to converse with. The population of sheep in New Zealand outnumbers humans seven to one. Generally, the conversations are one-sided, but at this point I will take what I can get.

It is almost five o'clock and I am still a ways out of Blenheim. A tough decision needs to be made here. Either I keep biking through the dark on a dangerous motorway. Or I swallow my pride and stick out my thumb for a lift. It's only about 50 more kilometers but I decide it's not worth the risk. I would prefer my ending be romantic. Road kill—not so romantic.

My thumb is displayed to any and all passersby, most of whom do not take my kind offer for company. To be fair, I am carrying a lot of baggage. But in comparison to the majority of hitchhikers, I would give myself at least a 5 out of 10 on the potential serial killer scale. The reason I am giving myself a five is because I am realistic about how absurd I must look. My cycling outfit doesn't exactly scream "out for daily exercise", my bike is covered in bondage by bungee, and my clip-in shoes have caused a frustrated look to be plastered to my face for the last 10 days.

So in my ultra-realistic approach to hitchhiking, I keep cycling while presenting myself to drivers. Every time I hear the distant sounds of a car coming from behind me, I stick my thumb out in excessive enthusiasm. It's kind of like Tinder, waiting to see if they have swiped right on you. A little unnerving, honestly.

Finally, a taker. A white pickup work truck passes me before pulling to a halt. Out hops a young Māori woman, early twenties. "Kia ora," I say with a beaming smile—attempting to look as non-serial killer as possible.

"Kia ora," she responds. "Where ya headed?"

"Blenheim."

"That's on my way. I'm not really supposed to take hitchhikers, kinda still on the clock. But if your stuff can fit, I'll give ya a lift."

"Thank you so much," I say, beginning to strip my bike and load it into the back of the white pickup.
"I'm Sequoia."

"Jess," she replies as we both elevate ourselves into the truck. Jess starts the engine and in a breeze, we are off.

"Lorde is really something," I say, listening to her latest song that's blasting through the speakers as we blaze the countryside that would have taken me hours to cycle.

"Is she big in America, too?" She must have picked up on my accent that has morphed American.

"She's big everywhere!"

"Yeah, the country is heaps proud of her, eh."

That's the beautiful thing about New Zealand, the pride for fellow countrymen. Because it's such a small country, its pride comes in powerful waves. Being here, I remember how far away from the rest of the world I really feel. It really is its own realm down here. Which can be isolating and freeing at the same time.

We remain mostly silent on the ride, listening to the tunes on evening radio. Jess is from the North Island and has been living down here for the last six months, working on the roads. Her dad passed away three years ago, and it's just her mum and sister left. Her mum was working two jobs, so Jess took this job, working the roads in the South Island. This way she can send money back to her mum. "It's kinda boring, but the pay's straight," she says. I can tell that her dad is a sore topic, she glazed over it so quickly.

"Do you miss him?" I ask.

"Nah." She rolls down the window and adjusts her outside mirror. I don't think the mirror needs adjusting; she just wants a distraction from the conversation. Either that or she cannot handle my lingering Rainbow Valley stink.

People deal with grief in their own way. Just because you didn't get along with someone, or because they were not a major factor in your decision-making, even if you don't miss them... doesn't mean you are not grieving. Grief is funny like that.

"We are coming up on Blenheim. Want me to drop you in the middle of town?"

"Right here is perfect." I thank her profusely for the lift. Waving goodbye, I begin to re-assemble my bike. *Ohhhh, shit.* I think. Literally, oh shit.

You see, when venturing into wilderness, I practice something called "Leave No Trace". The meaning behind this is simple: everything that we venture into nature with, we must take out with us. That means, no trash, no waste, no human feces should be left to disturb the natural cycle of things. With that being said, whenever I head into an area with no access to facilities, like the Rainbow Valley, I carry with me a wag bag or two.

What is a wag bag? you may ask. To state this as eloquently as possible, it's a bag that I shit in. This sealable silver bag looks like something you would take into outer space. It has an,interior layer of green plastic, and the bag comes with a chalky-like substance inside that reduces any odor. All quite well designed.

Following a defecation, the green layer is tied and the exterior is sealed… never to be reopened and only to be properly disposed of. If for some ungodly reason the wag bag happens to be re-opened… well, one can imagine the fury that is released!

So my *OhhhhShit* moment is literal, when I come to the fast realization that my wonderful wag bag is missing. Missing, as in it remains in the back of Jess's white work truck… #SorryJess

Chapter Thirteen

Confronting Conversations

I pull into the long winding driveway that leads to what was once Annie's All Natural Fruit Roll-ups. I remember eating those until they made me sick. Part of Dad having product sponsorship from them was an abundance of fruit roll-ups scattered in the house and van. They were ever-present on any family adventure.

Slowly cycling down the lane, I look around to see no sign of the company logo that used to be a staple in our lives. Just a long driveway, vineyards on my left and fruit trees to my right until, finally, a large house.

The house sits on my right, a barn-like garage on my left. I de-mount my bike and lean it against the barn. Looking around, there is a sense of familiarity to this place. I can feel my emotions start to bubble inside of me. Should I be here? Is it really necessary that I am here? What will it really accomplish? I take a deep breath and head toward the door. I look down at my already clenched fist; my almost white knuckles connect with the wood of the door. Nothing. I pull my hand back and knock again. Still nothing.

… Maybe it's not meant to be. Maybe a phone conversation with Graeme was enough.

My feet slowly make their way back to my resting

bicycle. Instead of leaving, my body sits down on the concrete platform that my bike is leaning against. I sit there, just sit. I do not want to move. I want to stay in this exact spot until Graeme arrives. Perhaps it will give me some time to get my thoughts together; it will give me some time to prepare what I am going to say.

There is a large round rock just below my foot. I give it a nudge to reveal its shape, almost an exact sphere. The size of a tennis ball. Light grey in appearance.

I remember now. I remember this driveway, I remember this barn. Dad and Graeme were talking business inside the house, and Denali and I were playing in this driveway. There was a rock.

I bend down to pick up the rock. A replica of the one Denali was playing with that day. This memory is vivid. Denali took another rock of a similar size, one in either hand, and smashed them together.

"What are you doing?" I said with my hands covering my ears.

"Look!" Denali said, holding out half of the tennis ball-sized rock, split directly down the middle. I un- squinted my eyes and leaned over to see the inside of the rock. Magic. Crystalized formations of pure magic.

Snapping out of my moment, I look up to see that a car is pulling down the driveway. A musky brown-colored car. It comes to a halt, and the door creaks open. A young woman in her early twenties steps out and turns to look at me.

"Hi," she says inquisitively.

"I'm just waiting for Graeme. Do you know where he is?"

"He's down at the other pasture. Won't be back for a few…are you Sequoia?"

I am a little taken aback.

"Yes."

"No way, it's been forever… It's Cabie! We used to play as kids. Me, you, and Denali. Wow!" Her enthusiasm is bubbling.

"Cool," I reply in monotone. My memory scrambling to place her. Graeme's daughter. I think she's Graeme's daughter.

"Well, you are welcome to hang out here, but I have to grab Thomas from daycare in about 15."

"Thomas?"

"Yeah, my son," she says, expecting me to know about her life.

I take a moment to think while Cabie runs into the house. By the time she comes out, I have made the decision that I would rather not sit on a concrete step letting my emotions fester while waiting for Graeme.

"Can I come with you?" I ask.

"To pick up Thomas? Sure, jump in." Her car is what you would expect from a mother in her very early wenties. Toys and lolly wrappers hurled about. A car seat, half secured in back middle.

We make our way onto the main road and into town.
"I remember I always thought I was going to marry Denali," Cabie says with a childlike grin.

"You and every other girl I know," I reply. She giggles.

It's true. For my entire existence on this earth, I don't think I ever had a friend or met a girl who didn't have a crush on my big brother. I want to be able to chat with Cabie, to make friendly conversation of our past. But the truth is, I have spent the last few hours, days, years thinking of this moment. The moment I was supposed to knock on Graeme's door, and there was supposed to be an answer. But instead I am sitting in a just-past-adolescent mother's car, heading to daycare to pick up Graeme's grandson. How the hell did this happen?

"I might punch your father," I say, half serious.

"That's okay," she says with a smirk. "I often feel like punching him, too."

I like this girl.

We pick up Thomas from daycare. Hands down

one of the cutest kids I have ever seen, and boy, does he know it. The three of us head back to the house on the land that was once Annie's All Natural Fruit Roll-ups.

"What happened to Annie's?" I ask.

"Oh, it went bankrupt," Cabie replies.

Karma, I think, then try my hardest to retract that.

"About four years ago actually. It was terrible. Mum and Dad lost everything. They officially separated. Thank God the bank couldn't take the house, so we still have that. But yeah, Dad met Choi, and Mum moved into the guest house with the guy she's seeing. Bit of a mess, but we pulled through."

"Oh shit, I'm sorry to hear that." I am actually sorry. Sounds horrific, especially for Cabie. "Who is Choi?"

"She's from the Philippines. Dad met her while he was over there and brought her back."

I laugh at this. I try not to, but it's just too funny to contain. I have been to Southeast Asia enough times to know that when a western man is going through a mid-life crisis, all he needs to do is show up to a Southeast Asian country, and within a few nights he has himself a post-pubescent distraction. It doesn't really matter the level of wealth, or in Graeme's case, none at all, for a chance at being taken care of by a western man seems too appealing to many SEA women. I am well aware of how those words sound. But the simple fact is, I have traveled enough to know that some stereotypes are stereotypes for a reason.

Upon arrival back to the house, we pick some fresh veggies from the yard and begin cooking dinner. It isn't long before Choi and Graeme arrive. I am in the middle of cutting a large freshly picked carrot when I hear them enter. I take a deep breath, and then put the knife down on the chopping board. Cabie delicately grasps it and says, "I'm just going to put this over here," placing the knife in the sink.

"Sequoia!" Graeme says with a beaming smile as if he is as daft as a piece of driftwood. He comes toward me to give me a hug. I duck the hug and hold out my hand for a shake.

"My golly, you've grown. A full beautiful woman."

"Thank you, Graeme, you have definitely aged." Subtlety has never been my strong suit.

"I wasn't sure when you were coming. So wonderful to see you!"

I nod and turn to the woman standing next to him. She is exactly what you would imagine. Very pretty, doll-like features, and the appearance of one in her late teens. In reality she was probably around 29 or 30... which for a man like Graeme, pushing 60... well, let's just say I am sure she keeps him young. I can tell by looking at Choi that she's a bit of a survivor.

Mum and me standing in front of the sequoia tree
planted at our old Christchurch home.

My Family.

Dad & Denali biking.

Visiting the Macpac Headquarters in
Christchurch.

In the South Island following Aspiring ascent.

David and Vicky at their home the night before
my departure.

Just before the departure from Christchurch.
Loaded up with all of my luxuries.

On the road from Christchurch to Waipara.

The necessities.

The Rainbow Valley.

All alone on the Rainbow (the camera was leaned against a rock to capture the photo).

The beautiful sights of the Rainbow Trail, Day 2.

More Rainbow Valley

Rainbow's End!

Sights of the Wellington Crossing

My Forest Gump, Rod, joining me for a long ride.

Rod and me on our break for lunch.

Hawke's Bay arrival. With my orange paniers.
Happy lady!

Denali, me, and Dad on the beach in Hawke's Bay '05

Climbing hallway in the Hastings home.

Raphelle and me in Hawke's Bay 2003.

Bittersweet goodbyes to Romly.

At a Marae in Hawke's Bay.

My big brother, Denali.

Taupo Bungy with Dad '04

Final night on the road – a spectacular sunset!

To be fair, I would guess she had to be. The kind of woman that would take an opportunity when it was presented. Even if that opportunity was 30+ years her senior.

The conversation through dinner remains civil.
"Sequoia, you are welcome to stay on the couch, and I can give you a ride to Picton in the morning," Graeme says, with a constant attempt to please. Cabie sends a leer my way, relating to her father's hopelessness.

"I think I'll just pitch my tent out front. Will be gone before the birds sing." My quick retort goes hand in hand with many of my sharp answers throughout the evening.

After dessert, as Cabie is preparing Thomas for bed, Graeme grabs his keys and begins heading toward the door. "Have to pop to the other vineyard to pick up some sample. Will be back."

From what I gather, after Annie's All Natural Fruit Roll-ups went out of business, Graeme parlayed their vineyards into something to do with the wine business.
I know that if I am ever going to get a moment alone with him, it is now. Up until this point I have carefully avoided any topic that could lead back to my frustration, due to the fact that I am trying to be respectful to his family and not pummel him like he did his business.

"I'm coming." I say, following him out. Cabie's smirk still lingers as she watches us head into the garage.

We hop in his old silver truck and begin to make our way out the driveway.

"So how has the biking been coming?" Graeme says as the old truck bumps down the gravel road.

He can smell my anger.

I cannot hold it in any longer. The words vomit-project from my mouth as my inability to contain my emotions overpowers my segue into adulthood. "I am still really fucking pissed at you, Graeme."

Pause.

"I know you are," he says. Pause. "I don't really blame you."

"What gives you the right to ban someone from their own father's funeral?" I am fuming. Tears are beginning to well.

"It was a difficult situation, Sequoia; I was put in a tough position."

"I DON'T GIVE A FUCK!" It's as if the anger were an ocean and has caused a tidal wave inside of my body. Flooding every inch of my emotion. Tearing through my eyes, through my pores. "You claim to be a friend of my father's?" I restrain myself from gouging his eyes out. "Then you should know that more than anyone else, my father would have wanted me there. I am his daughter—his only child left in this world."

"I know that," he interjects. But his voice falls on deaf ears.

"In life, you don't get to take these kinds of things back, Graeme. I will live the rest of my life with this. I will never have another chance to say goodbye." Tears are fully flooding down my cheeks.

"You know, Sequoia, I try to end every relationship every day in a positive light. That way if something happens, I am not left with a need to resolve it."

"Cut the shit, Graeme!" My anger that was beginning to simmer down catches a whole new fire. "We are not sitting here having this conversation because of the way I left home at a young age. We are not having this conversation because my father didn't know how to hold responsibility for his actions. We are not having this conversation because I was a 12-year-old child who was angry with her parents. We are sitting here, in this car, having this conversation because you fucked up." A heavy emphasis on the word *you*. "You, mate, no one else. You made the choice to pick up the phone call from a grieving young woman who had just lost half of her family, and tell her that she was banned from her own father's funeral." My ability to stay calm and classy has gone right out the window. "You fucking piece of shit!"

Silence.
Silence lingers.
The sound of his swallow reverberates.

"Honestly, I was hoping you would jump on a plane and fly down here."

Sharp air fills my lungs. I let it out slowly in an attempt to compose myself. A single tear touches my upper lip—in it I can taste the salt of my ocean. "I should have," I reply, beginning to re-register with tranquility.

"What stopped you?"

"You did."

"Oh."

We come to a roundabout and start the circle toward our right turn. "I was driving to work the other morning," he says. "The radio was on, just quietly. I heard the word *Sequoia* and turned the radio up. Sure enough, it was you. It's amazing the things you have accomplished. And now becoming famous."

Famous is an overstatement, but I do not correct him. It allows me a sense of superiority in a situation where I feel so utterly helpless.

"And this biking you are doing. Good on you. Your father would be really proud." Graeme's tone is parental.

"I don't need you to tell me that, Graeme. I am well aware of his pride." The truth is, I did need him to tell me that, I needed that from him. To feel as though I mattered in some way, that my presence was important to someone who treasured my father. Perhaps now he would see that my absence from the funeral was a mistake.

The truck pulls into an open concrete parking lot with large white industrial buildings on either side. We roll to a stop. Graeme's sun-dried face looks over at me, his sorrowful kind eyes hold pain of their own.

"I can't change it, mate." Our eyes connect, and I see with that look that Graeme, too, is still dealing with the grief of losing my father, his close friend. "All I can do is tell you how sorry I am. And I am. I really, really, am sorry, Sequoia." The glisten of a tear appears in the corner of his right eye. "Do you think you can ever forgive me?"

I wipe my tear-stained cheeks and swallow into my stomach. I take a deep breath, coming to the realization that my head is nodding. On its own. I have forgiven him. But I think it's just as much about forgiving myself as it is Graeme. He is a symbol, a figurehead, in this process of grief. A hurdle I must pass to further my understanding of loss. To grasp the concept of death.

As I attempt to wrap my head around this idea that they simply are never coming back, and what's left is emptiness, an unexplainable hollow echo inside of my soul. In a way it is similar to attempting to grasp the concept of the universe. When I was a little girl I would cry because I just couldn't understand how the universe could go on forever. It perplexed my every brain cell. There had to be an end point. Now, as an adult, I cry because I cannot understand how there is an end point… to life. How can someone physically be gone. Where do they go? How can my life continue on without the presence of this person?

Graeme picks up his samples, places them in the truck, and we head back to the house. Retracing our path around the roundabout, accompanied by just the hum of the truck's engine.

"I cannot explain where that came from," I say as we pull back down the long driveway. "I haven't gotten that angry in a long time. I couldn't control it, it's as if…"

"It's as if it wasn't you who needed to tell me those words?"

"Yeah."

Graeme nods.

"They stay with us, you know, after they leave this earth. A part of them will always be here."

"I want to believe that concept. I want to say that I know that… I do know that," I reply. I feel them, constantly. Sometimes one more than others, and each in different ways.

"Make painful choices now to have pleasure later."

"Pardon?"

"I tell this to Cabie all the time. Too many people make pleasurable choices in the moment that can

116

become painful later on. Smoke a bowl rather than go for a run. The painful choice is the run. It's those painful choices in the present that will be our pleasures later in life."

"It wasn't painful to tell you how I felt." I know he isn't speaking about this situation in particular. I know he is referring to life in general. But I still feel the need to tell him that it was a conversation I have been wanting to have.

"It was painful to hear it." From the driver's seat, in the parked garage, Graeme looks at me with a caring smile. "Painful, but necessary. I am really glad you came, Sequoia."

"Likewise," I respond.

I guess there is a bit of wise in this old man after all.

Chapter Fourteen

The Windy City

Three hours of morning riding landing me at the ferry dock in Picton, my last stop on the South Island before boarding the ferry to Wellington.

The Wellington/Picton ferry route connects the South Island with the North Island and is currently operated by two different companies. It takes me a while to figure out the difference between the two, as the dock is rather large. The Interislander service (the one which I will be taking) runs up to 19 times per week with a sailing duration of around 3+ hours, while the Bluebridge service runs a fewer number at about the same duration. I stroll about the hallways of the dock and gaze over the abundance of written history neatly framed on the walls. I begin to read.

"On 10 April 1968 the Union Steam Ship Company's roll-on roll-off passenger ferry *Wahine* capsized and sank at the entrance to Wellington Harbour. The disaster cost more than 50 lives and stunned the nation. However, for more than 80 years the 'overnight', as the Union Steam Ship Company called it, was a vital link in the country's transport network. The ferries were part of the Kiwi way of life, symbols of certainty and stability.

"Although many ships sailed between Lyttelton

and Wellington during the course of their longer voyages, a regular passenger service between those ports took time to develop. In the meantime, people simply took the next ship passing through port. By the 1890s, though, Wellington was growing rapidly as the colony's political and economic center. It was time for a dedicated service.

"The Union Steam Ship Company began cautiously. In April 1895 it advertised that its 31-year-old steamer *Penguin* would run once a week between the ports. Demand grew quickly, and sailings increased to two and then to three a week. Other Union Steam Ship Company ships redeployed to the service included the former trans-Tasman liners *Rotomahana* and *Mararoa*, which were running mates by the time nightly sailings were inaugurated in 1905.

"In 1906, the company ordered its first purpose-built Lyttelton ferry, the *Māori*, from its favorite builder, William Denny Bros of Dumbarton, Scotland. Just before he died, Premier Richard Seddon pressured the company about offering cheap tickets for his pride and joy: the planned Christchurch International exhibition, so the *Māori* was meant to impress. According to the shipping reporter who greeted the ship at the end of her delivery voyage, 'To sleep the sleep of the just or unjust upon the *Māori* is to experience all the opulent delights of purple and fine linen.'

"The *Māori* was big – 3399 tons gross and 107 metres long – but its engines made the difference. Instead of the traditional triple or quadruple expansion steam plant, the *Māori* sported new-style steam turbines. These were expensive to build and operate, but they were quiet running, an important consideration for an overnight ferry where the quality of sleep was all-important. (All subsequent Lyttelton ferries were turbine vessels.) The ship also featured bow rudders to make it easier to berth stern first, an unusual feature in the days before stern doors and roll-on roll-off ships. In November 1907, the *Māori* established a new record of 8 hours 46 minutes from Wellington Heads to Lyttelton Heads.

"Although original plans to decorate the ship's accommodation spaces with *Māori* motifs fell through, the 423 saloon and 130 second-class passengers still experienced a visual feast."

I was so fascinated by the history of the ferry crossing that I pulled it up on my phone via the WiFi onboard the Interislander. Eight hours is what it used to take. Now, on this ship where I sit, reading over the passage's history, I will arrive at Wellington docks in just under four hours. Not to mention I have WiFi, three decks to roam, glorious views, and a couple of cafés to eat my heart out on NZ's finest sausage rolls with tomato sauce. How times have changed.

Through the loudspeaker an announcement intrudes in a thick Kiwi accent: "Ladies and gentlemen, please make your way to your cars as the ferry will be docking approximately 10 minutes."

With that, the hustle and commotion of speedy

movements make their way toward the doors in passageway. Metal staircases lead down to the lower deck where my bike is sitting solo in a bike rack. I strap my laptop to my bike and, per usual, wrestle with my belongings as I bungee them to the back of my cycle. *I really have to get panniers.*

Following the line of cars exiting the bottom of the ferry, I reach the main dock. Pulling to the side of the traffic lane, I look up to see the crisp blue sky. A gust of wind sends a chill to my core as I zip up my jacket. There is no doubt I am in windy Wellington. I clip in to my bike and begin to cycle toward the city center.

"Wow, that's the lightest kit I have ever seen!" A boisterous voice with a thick Kiwi accent bounces toward me.

Stopped at a traffic light, I turn around to see a fellow biker with sturdy and strong legs like tree trunks and a torso that could knock you out with one punch.
Bikers have this weird nerdy lingo when they see each other. The flow of conversation becomes natural and inspirational for your future cycle journeys. If you're not up with the bike lingo (I am now becoming familiar with it), "kit" refers to the gear that is currently strapped to my bike with bungee cords. There is no question that this man is a serious cyclist.

"Yeah, I originally had a trailer but it just became far too heavy. I had to sort and ditch half of my stuff, and this is what I'm left with."

He laughs. "I'm just going to the grocery store and my panniers are bigger than your kit."

I am flattered.

"Do you know how to get to Tory Street?" I ask.

"Sure do," he replies with an enthusiastic smile. "I'm heading that way also. Follow me."

We make a left at the light and wind our way onto the wharf. One of the most beautiful views of Wellington is on the main boardwalk leading around to the Te Papa Museum.

"Where are you coming from?" he enquires.

"I started cycling from Christchurch."

"No way!! Up the Rainbow? I thought it was closed."

"It was," I reply, feeling pretty hardcore. "I had to lift my bike over the gates."

"Good thing you didn't have that trailer."

We come to a stop at Taranaki Street. "I'll let you off here then. Just follow that straight up and make a left. Do you mind if I take a picture of your kit before you take off?" He pulls out his phone in full cyclist nerd-out mode. "You don't even use panniers....amazing!"

I laugh to myself. I have been fighting with these bungee cords the whole way and want nothing more than a hardy set of panniers to hold my belongings, and here is a fellow cyclist admiring my bungee cord set-up. I smile for the photo and ride off on my bike.

The next morning, I wake up to my dreams of panniers materializing at the local On Yer Bike shop in the heart of Wellington.

"All we have are the bright orange ones. Both of them together will give you 35 liters."

"That will work," I say. "Thanks."

The bike salesman is a short stumpy man with a balding head and a twitch in his left eye. He has a loosely genuine energy as if he is interested in the world of bikes but not quite interested enough to be happy with his line of work.

"Where are you headed?" he inquires as he assists me cutting the tags off the panniers I bought.

"As a final destination? Auckland. But today, I am just trying to get to Palmerston North."

I am hasty in my response, not for lack of wanting conversation after the solo journey, but due to the fact that I am already late to be on the road and I know Palmerston North will take me at least eight hours to bike to.

"Are you taking the pass?"

"My plan was to take Highway One all the way out. It looks like it will be a beautifully scenic trip."

"You should definitely take Akatarawa Road. It's lovely and will also be heaps more safe because there is no cycle lane on the motorway."

"Really?" I look up from attaching my orange panniers to my bike.

"I have biked up it many times. It's a beautiful ride. Here, I'll show you."

He bends behind the counter and picks up a map, his enthusiasm for cycling apparent as his chubby face carries a passionate grin.

He places a map of the North Island of New Zealand and its many roads and offshoots on the counter, and his finger follows the line from Wellington up Highway Two and across paths through what looks like a national forest on either side. His finger ends on the west side of the North Island Motorway One—which leads straight into Palmerston North.

"This way you can avoid all of the cars on the motorway and the hills out of Wellington. The pass has one minor hill, but for the most part it's a beautiful ride." He sounds like he knows what he's talking about, and I track the map with the picture on my phone.

"Thanks a lot," I say, waving goodbye as I exit the store.

Before cycling off into the hills that await my

agony, I take a picture of my bike in all its new glory with the two bright orange panniers resting on either side of my back wheel. *No more bungee cords*, I think to myself with joy in my heart, *no more adjusting my belongings and stopping every five minutes to make sure nothing has fallen off. Just pure glory on the open roads.*

I set off around the Wellington boardwalk, looking back on its splendid view of this miraculous city. I have always loved Wellington, so it felt great to be in a place with familiar surroundings. The city hasn't really changed much. The architecture still stands, though maybe a new building or two is new, but the vibe in this city remains the exact same as if 10 years never passed.

Past the outskirts and into Upper Hutt I go. My anxiety about riding over the Wellington Hills has eased a little bit since my conversation. "You'll see a big sign that says Akatarawa. That's where you turn."
The bike salesman's voice resonates in my head as my eyes stay peeled for the next section.

Chapter Fifteen

Stranger Danger

Upper Hutt cannot come fast enough. The pannier peddler was seriously mistaken when he said that Highway Two had more room for cyclists. *Bullshit. I call bullshit.* The thought almost knocks me off my bike. A truck, very large truck at that, whips past my right shoulder. This is not what I would call safe riding. In fact, it is incredibly dangerous. I'll take two sketchy dirt bikers in the Rainbow Valley over this situation. At least there I knew what I was up against. Cars spatting left and right and no more than a meter of width between the concrete wall that lines the motorway and the hurtling traffic. I hold my breath for what feels like hours before reaching a signed turn-off to Akatarawa Road. With a sigh of relief, I take the turn…. I sighed a little too early because within a few kilometers on the pass, the hills begin.

I had been dreading the hills around the Wellington area, and thought I may have escaped them when the pannier salesman told me about this pass. "One bad section," he said. "One big hill and that's about all." One big hill, my ass. Unless the one big hill happens to fall in the first kilometers of the pass, which I highly doubt, then I almost guarantee that this is going to be a lot more challenging than I expected.

There is lush greenery in these hills that I haven't really seen so far. I will say, one of the spectacular things about my home country is the diversity in its landscape. From the golden hills in the Rainbow Valley, to the coastline in Wellington, and within only a few hours' ride, the rich deep greens of the Akatarawa Forest.

Three hours of biking this narrow winding road occupied by an abundance of hills leave me breathless. Just as I pedal my heart out to the top of one hill, another presents itself, like waves in the ocean. However, these roads are paved, so I cannot complain. And to be completely fair, there are a number of distractions that continuously present themselves. For example, a bush full of blackberries beckons me to pull my bike over and spend a good 10 minutes tasting the sweet burst of its fruit, leaving a hint of bitter as an aftertaste.

As my tongue is swirling with the memory of my last distraction, my tires are flying freely down the latest hill. I stretch my arms out to feel the wind between my fingertips. I am getting used to this bike; it is becoming familiar to me. To the point where I actually find myself doing things like yoga poses while cycling. Downward dog, for example, is a well-used pose on my morning cycles. A good stretch to start the day's ride. My comfort level increases, allowing for things like my current stunt—hands-free riding.

Pedaling along, I notice a beautiful pond nestled amongst tall trees on my left. Lily pads gently resting on the water. Moss-covered rocks border the pond, and some of the most exquisite statues

I have ever seen. Plantations of white stone, perfectly placed in this sanctuary. The strong and powerful forms of female and male torsos contrast flawlessly with the delicacy of the bordering flowers. *What is this place?* I wonder.

My feet have stopped pedaling at this point and my bicycle is coming to a rest. I apply the brakes and rest my bike against a wooden gate that leads into an open area of grey gravel. To my left is a path through the trees to the lily pond. Straight in front of me is a wooden fence with a gate holding a sign which reads "Sculpture and Art Garden".

I cannot stop myself even if I wanted to. My body simply begins to follow my feet, as they make their way through the wooden fence, down a verdant green path leading deeper into overgrown greenery. It's like something out of a mystical novel. No wonder *Lord of the Rings* was filmed in New Zealand. The landscape is so inspiring. Even the lily pond left me with the sensation of being transported into a medieval realm.

The trail leads to a small wooden bridge crossing the river below. It is also overgrown. The thought that I might be trespassing slips into my mind for just a moment... but as I reach the other side of the small swinging bridge, I cannot help but think that such beauty should not be hidden from passersby. Besides, the sign did say Sculpture Garden, and who would have a sign like that if they didn't want people to visit? The trail begins to meander up a small hill. It is definitely leading me somewhere. Lush forest slowly turns to a humanly maintained opening. To my right is

128

another pond, a smaller version of the lily pond off the road, and to my left a garden. In front of me is the most beautiful purple leaf plum tree covered with exquisite pink flowers. I think about pinching my wrist, just to make sure that I am still in some form of reality, but decide against it. Even if this is not reality, I think I would rather remain in this carefully crafted cosmos.

Eventually, I arrive at a wooden home with stained glass windows, a fitting fixture for the estate. I knock on the door.

"Hello." A deep and soothing voice sounds from behind me. I turn to see an older gentleman with kind eyes.

"Oh, hi. I am so sorry to just walk into your property, but I saw the sign."

"No, no, that's quite alright," he says with a warm smile. "I can show you around if you like."

"I would love that."

I follow the gentleman past another set of trees, along the winding trail and out into a larger open area. Slowly, I start to make out the many statues nestled in into the scenery.

"What is this place?" I ask in awe.

"This is Efil Doog Garden of Art." He brushes back a branch displaying more exquisite pink blossoms and walks me out into the opening of grass. "It's the life's work of Shirley and Ernest

Cosgrove, who designed both their home and their garden over these 11 acres."

"Eleven acres? Wow."

"Over the past 36 years they hand-planted more than 2,000 rhododendrons, along with countless camellias, azaleas, and other flowering plants and trees. They have transplanted numerous stands of flowers, nurtured a pine forest, built little bridges over streams on the property, and collected scores of outdoor sculptures." He is quoting from the website now.

"How magical." I say, following him around yet another pond and into a forested area.

"They say that these grounds would inspire Walt Disney himself," he says with a proud beam.

"So how did you wind up here?" Curiosity is overcoming me.

"We brought the place, my wife and I. Just a few years back." By now we are in a thick piney forest.

"Look down," he says. I look down to see fallen pine needles covering the ground. And then I notice a little head poking out of the brown mulch, and another one. As my eyes wander, I see hundreds of them all over the grounds of this thick forest. Little gremlin statues scattered about, almost creepy in appearance, covered in thick moss and staring up at me from their blanket of pine needles.

"We get lots of exotic birds here, too."

"It definitely has magic," I tell him. Magic is the right word to describe the feeling permeating me. A strange magic. A lingering magic.

I spend almost two hours exploring the grounds, statues, and the magic of Efil Doog Garden. Losing track of time often happens in mystical places.

When I finally say my goodbyes to the kind older man and head back out to the road, I come to the realization that two hours of my day have now passed and I was already pressed for time. I take a deep breath and mount my bike.

After another two hours of riding, the end is still not in sight. Another large hill is, though. It takes all my might and inspiration from my recent excursion to make my way to its peak. When I reach the summit, I unclip one of my feet and take a moment to soak in my day. To soak in my experience. To observe the beauty.

The sun is starting to fade on the horizon. *It was not time wasted*, I think to myself. *These are the experiences you must have while on an adventure like this, or else what is the point?*

I have about an hour of light left in this day. There is no way I will make it to Palmerston North by nightfall, not even by midnight at my pace. I make the decision to ride until I cannot ride any more, and upon darkness descending I will simply camp on the side of the road, like I have before.

Thirty minutes and a few ups and downs of hills later, I see a figure in the near distance. A fellow cyclist. I can make out black spandex. He must know what he is doing.

"Hello!" I almost shout toward him.

A little startled, the man turns around as I pedal hard to approach. He's handsome. Like very handsome. Not in the stereotypical clean-cut kind of way. More in the Kiwi lad kind of way.

"What are you doing out here?" he says in a cheery voice.

"I could ask you the same thing," I reply with a smile.

"I'm enjoying an evening ride."

"Likewise."

"Where ya headed?"

"Palmerston North."

He lets out a laugh. "Not tonight, you're not."

"What does that mean?" My stubborn nature kicks in.

"Well, it's almost nightfall."

"Yeah, I kinda noticed that," I say, looking up at

the darkening sky. "You live around here?"

"Just up the road."

"Can I pitch my tent in your yard?" Right after the words come out of my mouth, I realize it sounded sort of kinky.

"I'll do you one better," he says. "I've got a couch you can crash on."

"Okay." I follow him as he turns left and then heads up a winding road. "You're not going to chop me up into little pieces, are you?" My sarcasm is mixed with a hint of anxiety.

"That's impolite in this country," he chuckles. I can tell already that this handsome man is a kindred spirit.

Chapter Sixteen

Stranger Not So Danger

His name, Rod. His story… still figuring that out. After we arrive at his beautiful four-bedroom home, nestled in the high hills of the Akatarawa Forest, I jet-line for the shower so I won't repel him with my stench. He is kind enough to put some spare clothes out for me, as I mentioned that I had only one cycling outfit for my entire trip. That seemed to get a good laugh out of him. Following my shower, I make my way down the long hall from the spare bathroom, snooping to peek into a room or two on my way to the kitchen area.

The house is empty, strangely empty, and I can judge by the lack of décor, a woman doesn't live here. But the rooms have beds and what looks like women's clothes. As I walk into the large kitchen, I notice a string of photographs lining an open window that looks out onto the beauty of the rolling hills I just rode. The lined photos hang as delicate as silk drapes. I step closer and can make out the faces of a girl at all ages. But no, this is not just one girl, this is multiple girls. Different girls. His daughters. A total of five different faces smile back at me, strangers in their father's home.

"Good shower?" The enthusiastic voice approaches from behind me.

"Great shower. Are these your daughters?" He doesn't look old enough to have five daughters. The youngest looks around four, the oldest not sixteen.

"Beauties, eh?"

"They are. Where are they now?"

"With their mum a few hours up the coast."

I leave the conversation there. No need to pry into this very welcoming stranger. There is something about the Kiwi mentality that instantly allows you to feel comfortable in their presence.

"Ya hungry?" Rod asks.

"Starving. Can I cook, though? I haven't cooked in a kitchen in forever."

"All right… I'll risk it. We will have to run to the store, though. Got nothing in the fridge."

We hop in Rod's white pickup truck (I could have guessed what he drives—right down to the color) and head to the local grocery store. A strange sensation of cheating on my cycle tour waves through me, even though we are simply driving to the store and back.

"So you're heading to Palmy?"

"That's the plan… Then onto Napier and Auckland."

"So why are you cycling the country?"

I knew that question was bound to come up. "I don't know... I guess I just felt like a challenge."

"Napier's not exactly on the way to Auckland." Rod points out an obvious fact. *Here we go*, I think. Knowing full well where this conversation was leading.

"I'm from there."

"The Bay?"

"Yeah, Hastings actually."

"Never woulda guessed that." He's taken aback a little. I know exactly why. Ever since I moved to the States, I have almost completely lost my Kiwi accent. "How long you been gone?"

"Ten years."

"That's a minute. Ya family must've missed you."

I nod. I can feel it coming. That moment that I say what happened, and the entire conversation, the mood, and perception of me shifts.

"Your folks in Hastings still?"

"No, my mum lives in Afghanistan. She's working over there."

"That's not too close. What about your pops?"

"He passed away." The air starts to shift.

"Sorry to hear that." An awkward pause. "Any siblings?"

"A brother." Heavy air surrounds me. It's been four years since my brother's death, and I still struggle with how to answer the sibling question. It has taken me the last four years to feel comfortable in answering such a simple question. I have a brother. That hasn't changed.

"Where's he?" It may sound like Rod's asking a lot of questions, but this is a reality I face constantly. At one point or another, when meeting someone new, eventually the conversation will lead to family. Sometimes I can successfully avoid it for the first encounter. But eventually, I have to face this heart-wrenching reality.

"He's dead."

And there it is. The air has fully shifted. No matter who it is that I am holding a conversation with, there is always a moment where you can hear their heart break a little for you. I have become good at judging a person's proximity to loss, based on their reaction to mine. Those who have lost large in this lifetime have a sense of understanding for another's loss.

Rod lets out a sigh. "I'm so sorry to hear that. How'd it happen?" He's lost someone, too. Most people who haven't yet experienced a close loss are scared of the conversation that follows the original declaration. But those who know, those who have felt the depths of despair, know that it's a conversation not necessary to avoid.

"In an avalanche."
Pause.
"On the mountain K2."
Pause.
"With my father."
Pause.
"Four years ago."
Silence.

I can feel his gaze on me. "I heard about that." Compassion is carried with his tone of voice. I almost forgot for a moment that I was in New Zealand, a country where pretty much everyone knows the story. Their photos and the story were all over the front pages of the major newspapers in New Zealand when it happened. You see, when someone dies in the mountains, especially a mountain like K2, and especially a climber as well known as my father... the whole climbing community tends to hear about it. Given that New Zealand has a large climbing community, my father lived in this country, and it was such a dramatic ending—well, let's face it, it makes a hell of a news story.

"Very tragic," Rod says. His arm reaches out and rests on my shoulder. I look into his deep hazel eyes and the chiseled features of his face. It takes me a moment to realize the car has stopped. We are parked in front of New World grocery store.

We make an efficient run into the store, and I cart all the ingredients needed for a stellar dish. Departing the parking lot, groceries in truck, we head back to the house on the hill.

"It smells good," Rod says, entering the kitchen from the living room, where he has just put on the cool sounds of Eric Clapton.

"Want some wine?" I ask, already pouring him a glass.
The "smells good" statement refers to the aroma wafting from the stove. There are not too many dishes that I have mastered, but spaghetti was taught to me while living in Italy, and not to toot my own horn too often, but it is more than edible.

"So, why did you split up?" I say, waving my wine glass toward the strand of photographs. I figure we have gone into the conversation of death, why not approach divorce. Besides, I have never been one to beat around the bush.

"She broke my trust." His answer indicates he doesn't want to get into it. So I leave it alone.

After a full bowl of spaghetti (Rod has a second helping) and stimulating conversation, I follow him into the living room where a blanket is laid out on the couch. "You're welcome to crash one of the girls' rooms," he says, for a second time that evening.

"The couch is perfect," I say. It's the truth. After the last week and a half sleeping in a tent, a couch is heaven sent. Besides, it would feel a little strange sleeping in one of his daughters' beds. Technically, I am still a stranger although I sense we are becoming fast friends, but I get the sense that his daughters wouldn't be okay with it. Rod seems like he's trying to figure out what his life is now. My assumption would be he has not been divorced for long. The love for his daughters is obvious, but I cannot help but feel he is just trying to get back on his feet again. So, for tonight, the couch is ideal.

My eyes peel open. It must be around seven. I elongate my arms above my head and stretch my toes as far as possible. In the mornings, I like to imagine there is someone on either end of my body, pulling my hands and my feet in opposite directions. This allows me to wake up every inch of my body, to feel each vertebra in my spine.

Rod must still be asleep. He is not to be seen. I get dressed in my cycling gear, fill my water bottles in the sink. A pen on the counter catches my eye, and I pick it up and write a sweet thank-you note to a kind knight in shining armor... for riding in on a cycle and saving the damsel in distress from a darkening ride on Akatarawa Road.

Away I go, closing the door quietly behind me, as to not wake my knight. Just as I reach my bicycle and begin to wheel it toward the entrance to the driveway, I hear sounds coming from the garage.

"Leaving without so much as a goodbye?"

140

I turn to see a fully spandex'd Rod, standing next to his bike, a cheesy grin plastered on his face.

"Good morning," I say with a chuckle. "Where are you off to?"

"Didn't think I'd let ya bike to Napier alone, did ya? You can't even make it through the pass without me saving you." He's wheeling his bike toward me. It's not very often that I am speechless. But I am speechless. Napier is no joke of a ride—260 k's, give or take. It will take me a minimum of two and a half days to ride it. "The fact is, you have inspired me."

How can I argue with that? I can't. And I don't really want to…. The truth is, I could use the company.
"Okay," I smile. "But you have to keep up." These words roll off my tongue as my tires roll out of the driveway.

Chapter Seventeen

Forest Gump and the Gorge

I'm not going to lie—it feels good to have some company. Time moves so much faster when you have a fellow rider to converse with.

"It's nice to know there are still sane women out there."

"You think I'm sane?" I say in all seriousness. I have been called a lot of things in my lifetime; sane is not one of them.

"Stellar. It's nice to know there are still stellar women out there."

"Lost faith, did ya?"

"A little."

"Well, consider me a reinstatement of faith." I smile.

The majority of our ride up the coastal motorway has a shoulder that allows for us to ride side by side, evoking conversations of all shapes and sizes. There is something spectacular about the connection you can make with someone while undertaking a challenge. It's a connection unlike any other, perhaps because you are going through the mental motions of physical exhaustion, perhaps because it is a person just as crazy as you are for undertaking the task, or perhaps, just perhaps, it is because you are experiencing this feat together.

"I lost my dad, too," Rod says. "Was pretty hard. Didn't make it easier that there was a bunch of shit after he died."

"What do you mean?" I have a feeling I already know what he means. Generally, after a death, true colors are shown. What I mean by that is that people are in the shock mode of grief, they don't know how to deal. So when the important topics need to be discussed, like wills or assets, things can get very nasty.

"We had a family farm I used to run," Rod says. I can already see where this is going. And I know the frustration all too well. My father left a will when he was killed. No one presented it to me; I had to track it down. It was supposed to be probated by New Zealand Public Trust. When I finally got someone from New Zealand Public Trust to answer my calls, the assets had already been distributed. The bank account that was willed to me and my brother (containing more than six figures) had been emptied. Emptied by a woman my father had married. A woman I had met only once. A woman who caused the crack in my father's and my relationship to morph into a gorge. Needless to say, the entire situation got incredibly messy. Lawsuits and bad press messy.

A friend of mine once told me, "Death doesn't fix

anything." What he meant by that was simple: if a relationship is scorned after death, chances are that relationship was never strong in the first place. Rod's story of the family farm and heartbreak that led him to simply walk away was something that I had heard in one form or another from many a grieving individual.

I am not the kind of person to keep my frustrations to myself. When I believe I have been wronged, I make a point to do something about it. In the case of my father's death, I did not simply walk away from that situation. I was vocal about it—I did interviews, hired attorneys, even went so far as to work with a Congresswoman to create legislation to have the laws in the USA changed regarding the bank's obligations to deceased accountholders. I did this because the frustrating pain that particular situation caused me was an emotion I would never want a grieving child to have to face. With my vocal efforts came an influx of stories. Stories from individuals who had been through a similar experience, who thought they could open up to me on a topic that is not often discussed. It made me realize I wasn't on a wild rampage for no reason, that there was value in my efforts.

The day has flown by faster than I would have imagined. The next morning calls for a tough decision in trail. The decision of the gorge. A long, narrow, and winding motorway passes through an enchanting gorge. The issue? Well, I see none. But Rod raises the point of potential death by speeding car and lack of shoulder.

There is something energizing about the morning sun, especially when you make the decision to undertake a treacherous feat like the gorge. It's faster, you see. It will save us a good two hours of cycling, not to mention we can avoid the hills. God knows I have had enough hills on this journey so far. With an agreement to take the gorge, Rod and I begin a slow descent.

"Pull over up here for the lookout," Rod shouts from behind me.

I pull into a parking lot on the left side of the road. It has the appearance of some kind of tourist center. Large boards carry information about the local plant life, animals, and history of the area. Rod and I walk along examining the boards, then make our way to a small lookout point where you can see the depths of the crater below. Looking over the wooden beam and then ahead to the narrow winding road on the right side of the gorge, I turn to Rod and say, "I don't think your kids would forgive me if I got you killed riding the gorge."

Rod grins. "We'll be right. Besides, I'm really glad I came."

"Me too." I smile.

"You coming into my life is kinda like the symbol for how my life's gone."

"What do you mean?"

"I married young, was faithful, provided for my

145

girls. And then outa the middle of nowhere, I just got hit. Never saw it coming. Kinda like you. One day I'm just biking along and them bam, I'm hit with Hurricane Sequoia. Except this was a good hit. And my marriage... well, that was just a hit."

They say that the order of worst things that can happen to you are:
1. Divorce
2. Death (not yours)
3. Loss of job

Personally, I think it's a little ridiculous of a list. But it does put things into perspective, at least for someone like me... someone who has never been through a divorce. I would say I have taken a pretty big hit when it comes to loss—loss with regard to death. But with Rod's words, it starts to dawn on me that there are alternate forms of loss that equate to quite a hit in their own right. I cannot begin to fathom having your whole world ripped out from under you, like Rod had happen to him. Five beautiful girls left in the wake of an earthquake that took a piece of him. How do you even explain to your daughters...? Are there words?

I would think not.

The gorge is sketchy, like very sketchy. One meter max from the edge of the road to the railing that blocks a plummet down the gorge and into the roaring river below. Cars don't take it slow on these roads, but rather whip around the winding corners with no fair warning. Rod and I are single file, sticking as close as possible to the railing. It is beautiful in here, though. The gorge leaves an eerie impression—towering walls on either side, a mixture of thick mud and rock stretch up into the sky as rapids murmur below. You could lose yourself in this gorge. No wonder Mordor was underground.

Approximately two hours of sketchy gorge-riding later, and the motorway begins to open up again.

Having worked up quite an appetite, I see a spot ahead. We are coming up on a small bridge that overlooks a tame river. I pull my bike to the side of the road just past the conduit. Rod follows closely behind.

"This'll work," he says and we both lean our bikes against the metal ending barrier that blocks the cars from falling off the bridge. On the outside, though, so the cars do not cream our bikes while we are enjoying our lunch. Rod makes his way down the bank and toward the pacified river, while I detach our lunch from the bungee cords.

Last night, following spaghetti madness, we had an abundance of leftovers—gauging amounts in cooking has never been my strong suit. I packaged some of the spaghetti leftovers into a used Tip Top container and took it with me for lunch. In case you are unaware of the classic NZ ice cream that is Tip Top, it's delicious. But they are notorious for their containers, simple blue plastic and ideally sized for any leftovers. Tip Top containers are a staple in most Kiwis' homes. Thankfully, Rod's was one of them.

Pasta in hand, I head down the bank and look over to see Rod in the middle of the river. Not swimming, no, sitting on a little island made of rocks. In total the river is about 3-4 meters wide (hardly can be defined as a full river), with a simple stretch of cobbled island in the middle.

"It's an easy jump, Wonder Woman," Rod calls to me.

I smirk and take off my shoes, throw them across, along with a bag of other snacks I grabbed before departing this morning, and perform a dainty little leap, landing safely on the warm rocks of the island. After settling in to the ideal butt placement in the pebbles, I look around to see the waterway divided on either side of us, our quaint oasis parting its dancing flow. *How cool.*

The sun beats down as I open my knapsack of treats. Rod wastes no time on the spaghetti.

"Tastes even better the next day." He licks his lips.
I unwrap a hunk of cheddar cheese from a piece of wax paper, and reach into my knapsack to pull out a pocket knife. The knife was part of my foldable cooking set. Feeling like MacGyver, I unfold the blade and begin to cut into the sun-soaked cheddar.

"You're Kiwi as," Rod says, his eyes fixated on my knife, his mouth full of spaghetti.

"Sorry?"

"You're Kiwi as. Kiwis know their kit."

148

"Kit?"

"Got the kit, know your shit. All the gear, no idear," Rod's words rolling slowly and melodically off his tongue, followed by a chuckle.

I let out a laugh. That is flattery. My kind of flattery. For the first time on this trip, I think I know what I'm doing. It's a very empowering thought. I would rather be told that I know my shit than be told that I'm pretty. Always have. Always will.

Looking down at my phone, I see a message from David and Vicky. "Checking in. Hope the riding is coming along well!" In the bliss of the sunlight, I am ever-present in this moment of ideal company.

"You must have got a good message, with a smile like that," Rod says, looking over at me with amusement sprinkled with a touch of curiosity.

"I did." I will let him stay curious.

"I bet you have a whole bunch of guys sending you roses on Valentine's Day."

"I'm more of a tulips kinda girl," I say, throwing a wink at him. Over the years, I have become good at avoiding personal questions that touch on topics I'd rather avoid. Rod takes the hint and drops the subject.

After lunch, we pack up and remount our bikes, having only about five hours of daylight left before we will have to make camp for the night. The goal is to make it into the outskirts of Hawke's Bay by this evening, allowing for an easy ride through the abundance of farm land that leads to Napier. Those five hours move fast, a steady pace accompanied by more enticing conversation.

Chapter Eighteen

Vineyards A-calling

Hawke's Bay is the oldest wine region in New Zealand, and the second largest. Located at 39.4°S, in the North Island of NZ, the climate is maritime and similar to Bordeaux. It is New Zealand's leading producer of full-bodied red wines. Red wines dominate, with 88% of New Zealand's production (tons) of Merlot, Cabernet Sauvignon, and Syrah grapes in 2016. They also specialize in rich, complex Chardonnays. Thus says the blurb on the Hawke's Bay Wine site.

Believe it or not, I went the majority of my entire childhood/young adult life living in the bay and not knowing a single thing about its wine. It required returning as an adult, accompanied by a Google search, to learn some informative wine facts about the illustrious Hawke's Bay vineyards.

The wine country is ever present in the scenery when one enters the outskirts of Hawke's Bay. Vineyard after vineyard line the shoulders of the road and stretch into the distance. I learned back in Waipara not to stop for the pungent and tangy taste of wine grapes, or the concept of time will dissolve into the clouds.

The morning ride is short-lived, as distraction presents itself in the form of a coffee shop. I'm not sure the description of "coffee shop" quite does this place justice. It is an old wooden house turned into a boutique bakery and café. A country feel, with neatly packaged cookies for sale and couches to rest on. It's sweet on the tongue as well as the eyes.

The distraction in the form of coffee and a morning muffin allows me to gracefully slide into a conversation that I did not quite know how to approach.

"Do you mind riding ahead a little bit for the next few hours?" I ask a muffin-covered Rod.

"Ride ahead?" He looks puzzled.

"Yeah, I just feel like I need to ride solo for a bit." I wasn't quite sure how to explain the idea that this journey was done alone for a reason, and this part in particular—riding into Hawke's Bay—was a prominent part of that reasoning.

"Sure." He smiles. He gets it. No need for explanation. Not everyone clues in as effortlessly as Rod. Often, individuals in my life need a little further explanation when it comes to the stages of my grieving process. I think this presents itself for two reasons. Generally, those who need explanations for my actions are not familiar with the roller-coaster ride of grief. Emotions are generally the main thing that people question. For example, why am I crying in the middle of a grocery store when I see Milo? Milo is chocolate goodness gifted by the gods. A goodness that I used to bicker with my brother about. Not in an argumentative way, but in that tit-for-tat way that comes only with a sibling relationship.

The other reason people seem to need explanation, or reminding, rather, of my grief is because of my demeanor. I am a strong woman. I present myself with strength, both physically and expressively, and people tend to forget that I still feel. That my heart is still shattered with pain. Simply because I possess an exterior of vigor does not mean that my interior is not utterly lost in the wake of sorrow.

I graze the sun-kissed floral grounds of the bakery while Rod rides ahead. *No expectations means no disappointment*, I tell myself. It's utter bullocks— subconsciously we will always have expectations of a situation, place, or person. But if I can decrease my expectations, it may help. *Expectations of what?* you may ask. I have no earthly idea. I guess I expect the home I grew up in to still be there. That is one expectation.

My ride into Napier reflects that of my journey of loss. Inconsistent. Moments of gentle gliding, pleasant reminiscing, followed by periods of pedaling rage. Nothing novel in my thought progression; more a heightened re-cycling of sentiments. But needless to say, I found that accompaniment was imperative.

Rod and I reconnect at a roundabout leading into Napier's main town center, pedaling toward the round circle that divides Napier from Hastings. This morning I will be going to Napier. I will brave Hastings and my childhood home tomorrow.

Chapter Nineteen

Nostalgic in Napier

We cycle through the streets of Napier's town center, which resonate with Art Deco architecture. Memories of walking these cobblestone paths come to the forefront. In intermediate school, I attended Havelock North, as Napier was too far on the bus and Hastings was too sketchy. I remember the teacher took us on an Art Deco tour, explaining the significance of the town's re-building after one of the many earthquakes. According to Wikipedia, the 7.8 magnitude Hawke's Bay earthquake, also known as the Napier earthquake, occurred at 10:47 a.m. on 3 February, 1931, killing 256, injuring thousands, and devastating the Hawke's Bay region. It remains New Zealand's deadliest natural disaster.

Earthquakes have been a constant in the history of Aotearoa. In school, the teacher would drill us to mentally prepare us for if/when an earthquake hit. One of the first things to do was to find a door frame. Ideally you would stand in a deep door frame, potentially to shield you from the roof crushing you as it fell. Other instructional materials were pamphlets with detailed diagrams on how to mount shelves and paintings, and to secure windows to prevent as much damage as possible.

I say goodbye to my Forest Gump, giving him a long hug, which ends with "I'll see you soon."

Rod replies, "I sure am glad I was hit with Hurricane Sequoia."

I smile, and apply pressure to my pedals.

After my short excursion through Napier with Rod, the next point in my journey leads me to just outside of Napier, where I looked for a recreational building featuring a climbing wall. As a child we would frequent this wall. It was on the wall I formed vivid memories of this wonderful facility. It was in a warehouse, and had some great routes. I learned all about indoor climbing, growing up on those walls. The staff idolized Dad, and he would bring in kids from local schools and teach them all about the sport. Unfortunately, I found out through my brother's friend Shawn that the Napier Climbing Gym shut down a few years ago.

My vivid childhood memories of long days on the wall, and afternoons with fresh fish 'n' chips on the wharf became that much more present, now that there wasn't a chance to recreate them. During that conversation, Shawn also mentioned that Napier and Hastings were left with only a small recreation center as a gym. But he asked if I wanted to do a climbing session with him while I am in my hometown. Of course I agreed, which brings me to this small—and I mean small—climbing gym inside of a rec center. Shawn is waiting for me, a grin on his face and arms outstretched. This is the first time I have seen an old friend of my brother's, a friend from our home when we were in Hastings. I was always the younger, wild, and annoying sister. Denali always had a swarm of friends around him. Good guys with big hearts. Shawn was one of those guys.

"Oh, man, it is good to see you!" I beam throughout our hug.

"You, too. Been way too long."

Small talk allows us to get comfortable with each other after all these years. Shawn is married now, with a beautiful baby girl and another one on the way. We talk about my life, career, and this crazy cycle ride I am on. We put our shoes on, and Shawn starts with the first pitch, a warm-up. But I can see by his climbing style that he has maintained his visits to the gym after all these years, after the demolishment of the wharf warehouse. In our continuous banter, I learn that he recently went through a terrible loss of his own, the loss of his mother.

"Oh, Shawn. I am so sorry. How?"

"She walked into the ocean and never came back."
Some would consider this suicide. The truth is, she had multiple sclerosis. She was in pain and thought she was a burden to her family. So she made a conscious decision to peacefully saunter into the inevitable.

It begs the question in grief: Is it better to go in a way of choice? In a way of peace? I remember when my dog had cancer. Making the choice to put her down was the hardest decision of my life. She was my best friend. She saw me through some of the most monumental moments in my life. She slept with me every night and woke up next to me every morning. When Dad and Denali died, she was my emotional support, my rock. The decision to end her life was the right decision. It was the humane decision, for she was in pain. But as I held her head and watched her take her final breath, there was an unbelievable amount of guilt.

It is natural to feel guilty in loss. It's called survivor's guilt, and although it often refers to survivors of war or natural disasters, survivor's guilt plays a part in majority of people going through grief. I learned that with Dad's death. Leaving issues unresolved and words unspoken seemed to increase the guilt. But the circumstances that surrounded K2 were out of my control. The mountain took them, and there was nothing I could do about it. With my angelic Labrador, I consciously made the decision to end her life. And that guilt resonates deep.

Throughout our conversation about his mother, I wonder if Shawn feels that guilt. I don't dare ask the question, but I do not doubt it is an ever-present feeling in his grief process, as it is with mine.

"Want to try this green?" Shawn asks, referring to the climbing route.

"Sure," I reply, figure-eighting into the rope to which "green" referred. We cross-check each other, and I hit the wall.

My muscles are big. Too big. Bulky big. Not the type of fit I prefer. Personally, my climbing shape, alpine-style body, is what I prefer. All legs and lungs. The past 19 days of cycling have turned my body into a powerful machine; however, my thighs and booty are far from lean. The bulk is overpowering as I try to finish this small pitch of a climb. My movement is not fluid, but rather jarred and bulky. But it sure feels good to be back on the wall.

Chapter Twenty

Humble in Hastings

Long embraces with old friends minimize the loss of time between sightings. There are friendships that you know are for as long as you live. Raphelle is one of those friends for me. A person that I can spend ten years without seeing (or really communicating with, either), yet a simple reconnection brings our friendship right back to where we were before.

I spend my first night in Hawke's Bay at the home of Raphelle, a chance to catch up on the monumental and miniscule moments that have made up our lives this past decade. She is exactly whom I thought she would become. She had always carried a presence back in middle school, the presence of a mum, of an elder, even when she was just 12. I never doubted that she would grow up to be a principal or a teacher, and definitely a mother. Two beautiful children and a prestigious private school teacher position later, she takes me to her kitchen. Our high school friend Annie comes over to say hello and catch up on old times. A much-needed girls' night, after solitude and masculinity have occupied my recent time. Girls' night begins with cake-baking and ends with red wine-guzzling.

The following morning I wake to the sound of a three-year-old's voice. It's Romily, Raphelle's daughter, and she is in desperate need to come into her room, where I am currently sleeping (not anymore), to pick out her outfit for the day.

"Knock on the door, Romily, and ask very kindly." Raphelle's voice reverberates from outside the room's entrance. It's like *Frozen* exploded in Romily's room. The film that stole the hearts and television sets of millions of families around the world has definitely imprinted on Romily.

"Excuse me?" I hear, as a little head pokes its curly auburn pigtails around the door and peers at me with big blue eyes.

"Yes," I reply, trying desperately not to laugh. I have always been a sucker for pigtails.

"May I please come into my room?" Romily asks very politely.

Raphelle sure knows how to be a mother. It comes so naturally to her. She carries a vibe of stern but fair, loving but disciplined, comforting but not coddling. The morning moves smoothly, from Raphelle making breakfast and getting the kids off to their grandparents, to kissing her husband before he departs for the job site. The intimate inner workings of a young family. I simply soak it all in, knowing that it is not the life for me, but it is a beautiful life. Where the explorations are presented in different forms, and the emotional roller coasters are ever-changing. Where maturity is nurtured by parental responsibility, and the highs of life are presented in chocolate cake and pigtails. A life where the adrenaline is shot through goal-scoring at soccer Sundays, and connection is felt while seated at church. A life of adventure, a very different kind of adventure.

Raphelle and I get the day together, a day to reminisce. And it commences with a visit to our old high school. We also attended intermediate school together, and would ride our bikes from Hastings to Havelock North. That's how we first met.

At the time, I was living in a foster home in Hastings. Denali and I had been removed from custody of our mother and father, due to a number of reasons, one of which was allegations by both parties of the opposing being unfit for parenthood. While the courts spent a year determining that my father would be granted custody, Denali resided in the home of one of his close school friends, while I was in and out of temporary foster homes, one of which was just down the street from Raphelle's house. It took me a few months to admit to her that the home I would bike to every day was not the dwelling of my normal, white-picket-fence family, but rather that of a Child Youth and Family Services caregiver. Between seven and ten children/young adults stayed in this three-bedroom house. The number of troubled occupants would vary, depending on behavior and pending custody cases.

I kept my living situation quiet because of the look people would give me when they found out where my head would lie at night. The same look that appeared on Raphelle's face when I casually mentioned that I didn't live with my parents, but rather a court-appointed family. That look stuck somewhere between pity and curiosity.

My friendship with Raphelle far exceeded my time in the foster care system. It parlayed to the custody of my father, through a spell of living in Italy, and back to New Zealand for high school. Or at least a year of it. Our friendship saw us through my first love. Her cousin Alex Jay Scales.

I was thirteen when I met Alex. By then I had started noticing that boys were looking at me a little different. I developed early – let's just say my chest was not mosquito bites, and it was complemented by an athletic figure. I didn't really know what to do when boys would stare at me. Alex was the only one who really gave me tingles to my toes. He was goofy and cool, both at the same time. In the evenings after school, we would run together. He was the first person I felt like I could really talk to, to open up to. Our discussion topics ranged from him not liking school to our favorite types of music. Alex had a close group of guy friends, most of whom I didn't particularly care for. I only met them a few times, but always preferred to spend time with him, as just us. We would even spend prolonged moments cliché-ly staring into each other's eyes. His crystal blue, an ideal contrast to mine.

We had a solid four months together, crossing over into my 14th birthday. I remember the morning that I lost my virginity to Alex. The white sheer curtains waving in the breeze from the open window. I remember feeling that I wasn't going to ever forget that moment.

I didn't. Or I should say, I haven't. It was burned into my mind, sometimes painfully so. Because it is hard to think of Alex without pain.

On July 29, 2005, Alex, along with five of his friends, were speeding down a road in Hastings. Their car collided with a tree. It was a miracle that any of the boys survived. To my dismay, Alex was not a part of that miracle. He, along with three of the others, were killed that night. Late on a chilly Friday night, Raphelle lost her cousin, Judi lost her only child, and I lost someone who held a very special place in my 14-year-old heart.

I was thrown, thrown in a way I had never experienced, a way no 14-year-old should ever experience. Alex's death was the breaking point for my friendship with Raphelle. Alex's death was really the breaking point for many relationships and normalcy in my life. I rebelled against any notion of stability after he passed. I spun into a vicious cycle of troubled behavior. Desperate for any form of constancy. Desperate for my father (or brother) to try to understand what I was going through.

Just a few days after the accident, I remember attending one of Denali's hockey games. While I was standing on the fence line, watching my brother's natural athleticism shine through on the hockey field, another parent looked at my brooding face and turned to my dad.

164

"What's wrong with her?" I overheard.

"Oh she's just a little upset because she knew one of the boys who was in that car crash."
Breaking point.
The moment that infuriated me to my core.

My father, my own father, cannot even try to understand the fact that I am not just "a little upset." I will not just "get over this"—this has shattered my very gravity.

I didn't even try to communicate with my father following that evening.

My spiral took me from truancy to smoking. Late-night partying to almost expulsion, and eventually to a boarding school in Australia. My spiral took me away from Raphelle's mothering mentality and positive influence. It took me to my depths of emotion. It allowed me to experience grief for the first time, and turned my already tough exterior into a solid wall of steel.

"I'm really sorry about the funeral," Raphelle says to me as we stand over Alex's grave at the local cemetery.
I look down at the Spiderman tombstone etched with a picture of Alex. Preserved in time. Forever 15. The funeral she is referring to was Alex's.

"It's okay," I reply. I can tell she still feels guilty for telling me I shouldn't attend his funeral. What is it with me and funerals?

165

In her defense, Raphelle had no idea what he meant to me, no idea about the time we spent together. It was a confusing time for her, and she didn't quite know how to handle the family dynamics. Not to mention the overload of crying teens from the community. Teens who felt the need to attend the funerals of all the boys, with overdramatic tears drawn from their two-minute interactions.

I had the chance to say my goodbye at the wake. I remember standing in the ice-cold viewing room connected to the funeral parlor. I skipped school to go see him. Just me and him. The feeling of emptiness surrounded me as my lips pressed against his pale white skin.

"His death broke me," I say. "I don't think I would have survived Dad's and Denali's deaths if Alex's didn't happen. It prepared me for what it was to lose someone."

I can feel Raphelle's eyes fixated on me, but I don't part with my gaze on the engraving of Alex.

"I was really fucked up after him. With men, with my family. I didn't know how to grasp what life was. I couldn't understand the point of living." A single tear falls from the corner of my eye. "But with Dad and D, it's like the opposite. It's like, I have to live. I have to live every single moment that this earth has to offer me."

That's the thing about grief – it can bring us to our worst, or it can prepare us for our best.

Chapter Twenty-One

Whānau

"Here it is! Here it is!" I can barely contain my excitement as Raphelle pulls over the car in front of 21/23 Nelson Street. The small three-bedroom flat that housed some of my most precious memories with my family.

"Do you think anyone will be home?" Raphelle's question is valid, given that it's midday, midweek. The address is a clue to the housing setup. We occupied the second flat on the driveway; there were three total. And I can tell already that it has changed dramatically since we lived there. The fresh veggie garden that accommodated the front lawn is gone. In fact, any trace of grass is overpowered by the abundance of ordinary grey gravel.

There was nothing ordinary about the flat of my past. *Perhaps this was not the best idea*, I think to myself as I head toward the door, armed with my emotional support system, Raphelle. She too spent many an evening in this flat – pizza nights and hot tub parties.

My hand hits the glass sliding door. *Knock, knock, knock.* The door slides open to a wide-eyed, dark-skinned, beaming girl. No more than 10 years to her name. A wealth of braids in her hair, and an over-enthusiastic existence.

"Hello! Who are you?" she blurts.

"I'm Sequoia."

"Hi." She tilts her head as she says it, as if she is doubting my name is Sequoia.

"Is your mum or dad home?"

"My mum doesn't live here. She lives in Wellington," she responds, a little attitude showing through. She turns and walks away. I shoot a puzzled look to Raphelle, who is clearly amused by this whole situation.

"Hello?" A gentleman in his late 40s appears. It's apparent that we woke him from his rest.

"I'm so sorry to interrupt," I start, "but I used to live in this home, many years ago."

"You did??" the braided girl interjects, her zest flowing full.

"I did, when I was just a little older then you." I turn back to her father. "I was wondering if you wouldn't mind if I took a look around?" He is apprehensive, I can tell.

"Come on!" The girl grabs my hand and drags me into the house before the father can say no.

To my disappointment, it looks absolutely nothing like it did when we lived here. All of the incredible amenities that turned this house into our home were gone. But some remnants show through. The most recognizable of which is the blue wall in the kitchen, which Denali and I painted. As I enter the kitchen, I notice that some of the shelves that Dad installed are still there.

My hand follows the wall down the hallway. "What are you doing?" the girl asks.

"Well, this hallway used to have climbing holds on it."

"Really?" She is bubbling with excitement. "Dad, did you hear that?" she shouts.

"We installed them ourselves. The climbing wall ran from the kitchen all the way down to the bedrooms. So I would climb down to my room." I smile.

"Wow!" she exclaims. I can tell my cool points just sky-rocketed with this girl.

Raphelle and I say our thank-yous and goodbyes, and begin the drive back to her house. It has already been a pretty emotionally heavy day, so an evening with my mother will be a nice way to close it out.

My mother, father, and brother moved to New Zealand from Australia in 1989, just over a year prior to my birth. My mother was working as a choreographer for Kahurangi Māori Dance Company. She was the only *pākehā* (white-skinned non-Māori) to be invited to work there at that time. She held the job while completing her teacher training in NZ. As a result, Denali and I were also adopted into the Ngāti Kahungunu iwi.

The Ngāti Kahungunu iwi is organized into six geographical and administrative divisions: *Wairoa*, *TeWhanganui-ā-Orotū*, *Heretaunga*, *Tamatea*, *Tāmaki-nui-a Rua*, and *Wairarapa*. It is the third-largest iwi (tribe) in New Zealand by population, with 61,626 people (9.2% of the Māori population) identifying as Ngāti Kahungunu in the 2013 census. Yes, that's another blurb from Wikipedia.

A few weeks before I was born, Tama Huata, in consultation with his father, Te Mate Canon Wi Te Tau Huata, and my mother, granted permission to give me the middle name of Karanema, which means "first light of dawn".

Because I was born at 6:06 am on January 1st, 1991, this was a huge deal and I am incredibly proud of this entrance into the Ngāti Kahungunu iwi. It is a monumental part of who I am.

You see, simply being born in New Zealand is one thing, but being adopted into an iwi is something completely different. The Māori are indigenous to the land of Aotearoa. When Abel Tasman first settled Aotearoa, the British and the Māori came to an agreement.

Let me break it down for you, from text in *New Zealand*, edited by Wikipedians: On the 6th of February, 1840, a man named Hobson, who represented the British sovereignty, and about forty Māori chiefs signed the Treaty of

Waitangi at Waitangi in the Bay of Islands. Copies of the Treaty were subsequently taken around the country to be signed by other chiefs. A significant number refused to sign or were not asked but, in total, more than five hundred Māori eventually signed.

The Treaty gave Māori sovereignty over their lands and possessions, and all of the rights of British citizens. What it gave the British in return depends on the language-version of the Treaty that is referred to. The English version can be said to give the British Crown sovereignty over New Zealand, but in the Māori version the Crown receives *kāwanatanga*, which, arguably, is a lesser power (see interpretations of the Treaty). Disputes over the true meaning and the intent of either party remain an issue.

Britain was motivated by the desire to forestall other European powers (France established a very small settlement at Akaroa in the South Island later in 1840), to facilitate settlement by British subjects and, possibly, to end the lawlessness of European (predominantly British and American) whalers, sealers, and traders. That being said, officials and missionaries had their own positions and reputations to protect.

Māori chiefs were motivated by a desire for protection from foreign powers, the establishment of governorship over European settlers and traders in New Zealand, and to allow for wider settlement that would increase trade and prosperity for Māori.

So in my opinion they got screwed over by the British. The majority of indigenous communities which were "settled" by the British were pushed onto tiny sections of land called reservations or missions, to pretend they didn't exist. In comparison to the Native Americans and Aboriginals, I would say the Māori are doing pretty well. With that being said, I would add that the Māori in no way have received fair treatment in relation to their land rights in New Zealand. However, I will give New Zealand credit for the fact that there is more integration of indigenous culture in a way that very few, if any, western countries have done before.

My mother has been a huge advocate for indigenous rights, not just in New Zealand, but also with her work on the Native American reservations in the United States and with the Aboriginal community in Australia. Thankfully, she maintained positive relationships with Ngāti Kahungunu iwi, as I have had a desire to reconnect with those roots.

My mother and I drive out to the Kahungunu Wairoa Marae to attend the latest show by the Kahurangi Māori Dance Company. Today's performance features a look back at the life of their grandfather and elder, the late Canon Wi Te Tau Huata, who was a prominent leader in the iwi, an Anglican priest, and also a friend and supporter of my mother.

Being back on the Marae with whānau that I haven't seen since I was very young brings a feeling of comfort. I honestly don't remember any of the faces that I see, for I was far too young for

172

my facial recognition software to have an effective memory database. But it doesn't make a difference; I am welcomed with open arms.

This is one of the incredible aspects of the Māori culture, their welcoming nature, their ability to make you feel like you are in the presence of whānau (family). Our embraces consist of touching foreheads and noses while holding the embrace. A position which far exceeds the quick connection of a hug or a kiss on the cheek. The Māori greeting presents an immediate intimacy and clear connection with another human being.

The performance is everything I would expect from a powerful story and equally powerful presentation. Story-telling through the form of traditional Māori dance integrated with modern styles. Tribal tattoos are displayed on the dancers' skin, adding to the authenticity of the performance. Māori are strong, and their strength resonates through their performance about the life of Te Mate, Canon Wi Te Tau Huata. My mother's pride is also evident.

Chapter Twenty-Two

Bungee of Abyss

With the morning sun comes emotion for the adrenaline-filled day. A smooth but hilly ride from my drop point in Napier, then onward into Taupo. My frustration from my mother's lingering words resonate through my ear drums, giving me motivation to grind forward in my hilly pursuit.

In the wee hours of the morning, my mother generously offered to give me a ride in her rental car to a drop point outside of Napier. The first few hills, coming out of Napier heading in the Taupo direction, can be incredibly dangerous. So I took her up on her gracious motherly offer, without telling her that over the last few weeks my exploits have much outweighed the treachery of the Napier hills.

It wasn't but fifteen minutes into our departure from Raphelle's beautiful Hastings home that my mother began to steer our conversation in a direction I did not want it to go. The direction of my father.

My mother and father have been divorced for many years. They did not speak for many years. They were not a part of each other's lives in any way, shape, or form. Like many divorced couples, my mother holds ill will toward my father. That is a bit of an understatement, but I am sure you get the drift.

Therefore, when it comes to the topic of my father, quite frankly it is not something I ever feel I need to discuss with my mother. Not a subject that I wish to hear.

I suddenly come to the realization that my mother didn't offer me a ride out of Hawke's Bay just for the sake of the hills. She offered it to me so she could be alone in a car with me and bring up a conversation that I did not wish to have.

After approximately another ten minutes of attempting to block out comments she is making about my deceased father, I have finally had enough.

"Stop the car, please. Thank you for the ride, but I will bike the hills."

"Sequoia, you are running away from your problems." Her tone is commanding.

"No, Mother. I am choosing to not sit here and listen to you. There is a difference."

"You need to understand some important things. Your father was a bad man. He made up allegations about me, saying I was crazy."

"How about you pull over and let me out of the car?" I am trying to remain calm. The wheels begin to slow; her voice does not.

"You need to hear this, Sequoia."

"Actually, I don't," I say, while opening the door of the now slowly moving vehicle. My chance to escape.

"Sequoia, I am your mother."

"Yes. And I thank you for birthing me, but at this current moment I would rather brave the dangerous hills of the bay on my cycle than listen to this any longer." By now I am collecting my bike out of the trunk of the car. "There is a reason I wanted to be entirely alone on this trip. A reason I asked you not to join me in Hawke's Bay. But you didn't listen. It was too hard for you to just respect what I asked."

I shut the trunk of the car, hear some commotion coming from the driver's seat, and then watch her speed off.

Taking a deep breath, I mount my sturdy cycle and begin to pedal.

The reason was simple. I did not want her sharing the experience of Napier with me because it was not hers to share. I shared a home with my father and brother. A home and memories that are imprinted on my mind and childhood for the rest of my life. No toxicity in someone's words can take that away, not anyone's words, not even the words of my own mother. But that does not mean I have to remain docile while she spews the toxicity of her involvement with my father.

The simple fact is, I already know everything she is going to say. Perhaps she's right, perhaps I need to hear it. Not for the sake of actually hearing it, but for the sake of letting her say it. As a daughter, to a woman who has lost her other child, her firstborn. Perhaps I can simply hear what she has to say. I want to have that level of compassion. I desperately want to have that level of compassion.

But this is not the time, or the place.

This journey is a part of my way of grieving. I need to be allowed to grieve in my own way.

Thankfully the overflow of emotions is pushed out through the looping pedals. I pour my anger and pain into a circular motion. This seems to bring a calming sensation after a period of time. It's a meditative motion that allows me to glide over the hills into the spectacular scenery that is the Taupo area.

Upon my arrival in town, I lean my bike against a concrete bench that looks out over the crystal-blue water that makes up Lake Taupo. It is a clear early afternoon, and the lack of clouds reveals the distant figure of Mt. Ruapehu. Ruapehu is an active stratovolcano at the southern end of the Taupo Volcanic Zone which includes two ski resorts that Denali, Dad, and I would frequent often.

Today is April 27th. It is the day of my brother's birth. Strange to think that time stands still for those who have passed on. This day would have marked his 29th year on this earth.

"Every year she has a birthday for Alex." Raphelle's words ring out in my mind. "I find it a little strange."

In a way, I understand why Judi would want to celebrate the day of her son's birth even though he is no longer with us, like my mother does for my brother. Whatever someone needs to help them grieve and help them live their life.

I remember two years after Denali was killed, a group of us gathered in San Francisco and we all sang him *Happy Birthday* for what would have been his 27th. I was sitting on a chair in the corner of the room of the Zen Center, and still remember feeling incredibly awkward about singing a birthday song for someone who no longer lived on this earth. A person's birthday symbolizes the amount of time since they were born that they lived on this planet. If they are no longer on this planet, how can we continue to celebrate as though they were still here? My inner cynic constantly questions these notions, while my compassionate side tries to understands that some grieve in different ways than others.

I open my phone's Facebook app to see that my mother has posted some old photos of Denali, wishing him a happy birthday. I close the app and place my phone in my purse. Zip the gold zipper of my black evening bag and place it in my bike's panniers – the symbol of my opposite worlds connecting. My panniers are loaded and off I go up the hill of Taupo, onto the awaiting thrill of a bungee jump. Bungee cords seem to be a constant in this journey of mine.

178

Towering 150 meters over the Waikato River is the Taupo Bungy. This is not a jump for the faint of heart, nor is it a jump that is unfamiliar to me. I first did this freefall when I was 12 years old.

My father, brother, three of my brother's friends, and I were on our way to go skiing. Like many of our skiing trips, we would spend the first night camped in Taupo by the hot springs, to enjoy a soak as a pre-requisite for skiing. It always seemed to be a hoard of smelly teenage boys and me, piling into Dad's van. This time was a little special, though; this time Denali would be doing the bungee jump that we had all driven by a hundred times but never tried before.

I watched my fearless brother take a swan dive off of the bungee, a perfect swan dive before he was dunked in the tranquil river below. I looked up at my dad. "I want to do it!" I say with full confidence.

Kind of like the confidence I carry right now as I make my way to the window to pay for my jump. Unlike 14 years prior, my confidence as I make my way through the gate for "Jumpers only" and head down the long bridge will remain intact. I sit in the exact spot my gluteus maximus previous occupied, and go through the exact same procedure where the operator runs me through the instructions. The only difference being that this time is a solo jump, and my previous adrenaline rush over the Waikato River was a tandem with my father.

"When you are finished being tied in, wiggle on over to the edge. Put your hands above your head and just lean over," the operator instructs. *Lean over? Yeah, bullshit. I'm going full Denali-style.*

"Ready?" he says, and I begin to wiggle. *Oh NO,* I think as my tippy-toes creep to the edge of the daunting drop. This was the exact moment that all my confidence was vacuumed out of me on my previous attempt to be a badass. My whole body swiveled into Dad, my arms wrapped around him, my head turned into him, as to not see the void. "I changed my mind," I whimpered into his bearlike chest.

"No way, mate," he said. His hands gently but forcefully grab my chin, pulling my hidden face toward his. Eyes tilted up at him, his gaze did not waver. "You got this, hear me? You got this." I took a deep breath, like I am right now. I held onto my father with all my might.

With that moment in my mind, my arms form into a swan dive position above my head.

"3….2…..1…….BUNGEEEEEE!"

With dad I screamed all the way down.

Now, a perfect swam dive executed in quiet flawlessness.

I had never held my father tighter than in that moment. The then and the now in one, if only for a split second of recollection.

Chapter Twenty-Three

Retreat of Backpackers

An early dinner settling in my stomach, the sunbeams beginning to ricochet off the lake's glistening water, and for the first time on this journey of solitude I actually feel alone. Maybe being surrounded by people reminds me of the joys of interaction. Most of my trip has been spent on the seat of a bike, or in the country, not having constant reminders that there are other human beings on this earth. Unlike now, where I sit at a table that possesses an awe-inspiring view of Taupo Bay, surrounded by the chatter and laughter of friends and family enjoying each other's company. Getting lost in the folds of friendly people reminds you that sometimes you just need someone to chat to. A Backpackers is the ideal place for it.

The solidarity of the moment makes my decision for me. Tonight I shall not camp; tonight I shall seek a Backpackers or hostel. They're not hard to find. In New Zealand they are almost as common as the Starbucks on every corner in America.

I see a sign that reads "Urban Retreat Backpackers" and make my way inside. "Kia ora," the German girl behind the counter welcomes.

"Good evening! Do you have any beds available?"

"Yah." Her accent is even thicker in English. "We have private das is $25. Unt semi-private, das is $17, and unt bunk das is $7."

"Bunk me on up," I smirk. She doesn't get it. I clear my throat. "One bunk bed, please."

Why on earth would I ruin the whole point of coming to a Backpackers, unless I'm going to be all mixed in with the penny-saving college kids who possess an innate ability to make me feel ancient in my 26 responsible years? This is what I came for, interaction to the extreme – one night of it – before I ride in solitude to Tauranga, Hamilton, then onward to Auckland.

The nice German greeter hands me a key and a blanket. "Down ze hall, to ze right."

My inner snobbery wants to give the blanket back, but after sleeping in my own stench in the Rainbow Trail for four days, what's a little potential cum stain on an overused blanket?

The evening turns out just as planned. When in need of good company and a few laughs, always seek out a Backpackers.

"So I stripped down butt naked…," Adam says in his thick Australian accent. He's in the middle of telling a hilarious story about being stranded in Tanzania.

"You did not," Shelly interjects. She's from France, 22 if I had to guess. Pretty and petite.

"Oiiimamai, let him tell the story," the bombshell Columbian pleads. Her voice is melodic and she has an uncanny resemblance to Sofia Vergara.

The truth is, I have reached a point in my life now where I usually find myself alone in a nice hotel room, with all the amenities, including privacy. With privilege comes privacy. But sometimes I don't want privacy. Sometimes I prefer a community environment, bunk beds, and lively conversation. Sure, you have to sacrifice hygiene in the unisex bathrooms, but in the grand scheme of things, it is well worth it for one night of interaction with likeminded wandering souls.

The group I enjoyed this evening's festivities with were just that – likeminded. Each person was from a different country, a different way of life, coming together on their journeys to trade travel stories and relish in good company. You don't get this kind of interaction staying in an amenities-filled hotel with a pricey view. This kind of connection can be found only when wandering.

Knowing I have a full day's ride to Tauranga, I say my goodnights and head to my assigned bunk. I am sharing the room with five other girls and choose to take the bottom bunk closest to the door. Many years ago when I was in Thailand, one of girls sharing my room snored so loudly it caused the entire room to rumble. I learned my lesson that night, to always be close to the door in the event an easy exit is necessary.

Earlier in the evening, I had caved on the blanket and retrieved my sleeping bag from my panniers, which were stored with my bike in a locked closet. I figure it's a safer bet for my immune system to sleep in my own bag; besides, it has been my constant companion these last few weeks.

Curling into my sleeping bag, the confinement of a bunk bed surrounding me, my eyes focus on a series of black squiggles on the panels of the bed above. *This is going to be good*, I think to myself. For only in a hostel can you find supremely amusing graffiti.

Written in permanent marker on the bunk bed's wooden slats are a series of quotes:

> "Follow your feet, ignore your head."

> "Happiness is only real when shared."

> "No Regrets!"

And my personal favorite …

> "Love is like farting. If you have to force it, it's probably shit."

With a subdued chuckle at the last quote, I close my eyes and drift toward dreams, hearing a lullaby in the snores.

Chapter Twenty-Four

Caught between Now and Loss

Grief seems to be a constant on this journey. Wherever I turn there appears to be some reminder of the continuous process of loss.

In Tauranga, I have the chance to meet up with Judi and Paul, the mum and step-dad to Alex. The weathering of constant grief is evident in Judi's eyes. But she is still able to talk about Alex with a smile, even though her voice may quiver from time to time.

She asks me a series of probing questions, grasping for new moments of her son's short time on this earth. Completely understandable.

I am in Tauranga for only one night, but I awaken with an awful feeling in my stomach. A feeling I can't quite place. I sit up in my sleeping bag, clenching my abdomen in an attempt to figure out if it is an intestinal issue or an emotional one. I get odd feelings sometimes. Not often enough to cause concern, and sometimes they mean nothing. Or, in the case of today, my strange feeling raises the question of whether spiritual abilities open my cosmic connection far more than I realize.

From the moment I hop on my bike, things start to go wrong. It commences with my chain needing to be remounted (not the first time on this trip), then it starts to rain, and rain hard.

Following the hard raining, and as I am exiting Tauranga, my tires slip out on the pavement, causing me to lose my balance then take a little tumble. By the time I exit the town's center and am approaching Mt. Maunganui's main roundabout, my emotions are at the height of aggravation. Every little thing is causing frustration: the one piece of hair sticking out of my helmet and tickling my cheek; the splashes from the cars' tires that constantly cover me with new splatters of dirty water; the Kiwi drivers' inability to notice me on a bike.

The roundabout is about double the size of most of the others one would usually come across in the towns and cities of Aotearoa. It has a large circular median that divides Mt. Maunganui from Tauranga and the main motorway. There is no side path for bikers on this road, no room to signal without exaggerated arm movements.

Stopped at the entrance to the roundabout, I perform an elaborate arm movement to indicate my intent to cycle around and exit to the main motorway that will lead me out of town. Out of the middle of nowhere I am hit. Grazed on my right side, down I go, hard and fast. Thump. My head.

My eyes wince open and a sharp breath enters my lungs. Pain. I feel pain. Where is the pain? I move my neck. I wiggle my fingers and my toes. Those are okay.

"Shit. Shit. Shit. You okay?" I hear a fumbling accent. Broken English. I tilt my head and look up to see an older man.

"Ummm, I think so…," I reply. To my surprise my feet are still clipped into my pedals and with that realization my gaze lands on my knee. My knee which holds the full weight of the bike, my knee which is bleeding. I instantly unclip my feet, and the man assists me in pulling my bike off my knee. How ironic that I continue to complain about Kiwi drivers and I am nicked by what appears to be a non-Kiwi.

"Shall I call police?" he asks me, riddled with fear.

"Honestly, I think I am okay."

After I assure him of my ability to recover and I drag my bike to the side of the road, I do a few movements with my knee to test my ability to ride. It feels okay.
Within a kilometer I come to the fast realization that it is definitely not okay. Searing pain causes me to cease riding and face the hard fact that I may have seriously damaged my knee.

"You are going to have to stay off of it," the white-haired doctor tells me. "I mean it. At least a week."

"I can't do that," I tell him insistently.

"Well, if you want it to heal, and you do not want to risk permanent damage, then you will heed my advice."

It takes me a moment to let his words sink in. I am in my mid-20s; I cannot afford to permanently damage my knee. I may be persistent and stubborn, but I am also logical when need be.

I hobble to a hotel. The kind of hotel offering privacy and panoramic views. The kind of hotel that will offer me soft pillows to soak my sorrows.

Chapter Twenty-Five

Nameless

There's a man. To prevent a defamation lawsuit, he shall remain nameless. This nameless man and I had shared one of those strange relationships that most would find hard to wrap their brain around. A separated togetherness that would send most women into a headspin. Don't get me wrong—I have had my moments of headspin with him, but I also realize with both of our lifestyles, the situation was kind of ideal. When we were together, it was incredible. Two, sometimes three days every month or so. Between his climbing expeditions and my adventures, we managed to find a few moments to be in each other's arms. There were moments of true intimacy with this man. Moments where I would lay my naked body against his chest, and hold his heartbeat in my hand. Short-lived moments between the whirlwinds that were our lives. But they were pure moments, they were true moments. The kind of moments that make you stop and think about what our purpose is on this earth… if we are meant to find another.

Over the period of two years, this nameless man had fast taken over my thoughts, especially when I spent time in solitude. A reel of our moments would loop when my mind would wander.
Nameless is a unique man.
Fantastically unique.

One of the most amazing men I have ever known.

But he was always good at leaving questions unanswered. Was selfish beyond belief. A trait my father also possessed. A trait many, if not all, mountaineers must possess in order to survive. A trait I also possess, if not more so than him.

Nameless was terrible at communication—beyond the stereotypical male's inability to communicate—I mean really terrible, and constantly left me questioning where I stood in his life. I presume he often wondered about my position correspondingly, seeing as my contact was also inconsistent. We were both unwavering in dedication to our own path, unwilling to compromise, held in a cycle of selfish notions. The timing was not right. Or perhaps the pull not strong enough.

There are very few people in this world who can awaken my inner "housewife". My natural nurturing mentality that's buried beneath a tough, pushy exterior. In the small spate of time spent with Nameless, my nurturing nature slowly presented itself more and more. To the point where, our last weekend together, I prioritized his schedule and feelings over my own.

We had exactly two days together at my home in Los Angeles before he left to climb Everest (again), and I left to cycle New Zealand. He had just come back from an expedition and was exhausted. I had a pile of paperwork on my desk, and a stack of equipment to sort, but my focus, my attention, was on Nameless. I began to cook a healthy dinner for us. Nameless lay down to rest his eyes. I could tell from the moment he entered the room how tired he was.

While my knife cut through the garlic clove that was being minced as glaze for the salmon, I looked across the open kitchen of my apartment to see him sleeping on the bed. Face up, hands folded on his chest, peacefully resting. In that moment I began to smile.
That was the moment I realized I was falling in love with Nameless.

It was something I would probably never tell him. It took Nameless a year of us half-heartedly together before he could say the words "I miss you." To most women, or people for that matter… that would sound absurd. But there was something that felt so right about hearing those words. He didn't throw words like that around. So when he would say something sweet, I knew he really meant it.

I think it's a part of my nature that when things come easy to me, it takes away from the satisfaction. There was nothing easy about Nameless. Intimacy issues do not even begin to describe him. He was hard to read, aloof, and rarely said the right thing. His barrier as thick as the Great Wall of China, and no matter how close we got, I could always sense that wall. I often question why someone who came from such nurturing and simplistic background could be so guarded, and why my broken past still allowed me to love. These ponderings may seem squint-worthy, but these were all attributes in my eyes. All more reason he continued to occupy my thoughts.

In this moment, I am broken, not physically (thank God) but emotionally. I set out to do a task, something I trained and prepared for. Something I sacrificed time for, money for, my body for... and now I may not be able to complete it. The ultimate feeling of defeat. To add insult to injury, I am alone. Alone in a country that is haunted with the ghosts of my past. I look down to my swollen knee. Tears well in my eyes, and loneliness echoes on the white walls of this hollow room.

The only voice I want to hear is Nameless's. Just the sound of his voice can bring me comfort.
I know he is aware of my accident.
No call.
I know he has service where he is....
No call.
I know he cares....
No call.
So I call him......
No answer.

I cannot do this. I cannot be in love with someone who doesn't love me. How can I be so strong in the face of danger? So tough when presented with a challenge? How can I be so fearless in my demeanor ...so powerful in my presentation, but be so broken by a man who remains nameless?

The most basic of human emotions has crushed me, far beyond the bike falling on my knee.

Chapter Twenty-Six

Wallowing in Strength

Fuck buses. I shouldn't say that. The bus is technically saving my behind. But seriously, fuck buses.

Because I want to be as easy as possible on my knee, and it happens to be my driving knee, I cannot operate a car. And because I am stubborn and insisted I do this entire journey without any support crew, I am left waiting for a bus. A glorious bus. A big beautiful glorious fucking bus. In case it has taken you a moment to clue in, the injury from my knee has dwindled my spirits to the point of no return.

Last night I went past the point of feeling sorry for myself, and into the point of anger. I wonder if the seven stages of grief can be applied to a bung knee.

I had a friend who was all set to play professional ball back in the States. He was in one of the top universities and was slated to go in the first round of the draft, but then he was injured, seriously injured. He lost all hope of returning. His whole life was spent working up to that moment and it slipped through his fingertips. He lay in bed for weeks. His family didn't know what to do. That is a kind of loss. The loss of a dream. It's understandable that he didn't know how to deal with his grief. I am one day into a non-permanent injury, and I sense that I am in the depths of despair – I can only imagine what it must have been like for him.

The bus arrives three minutes late. I politely ask the driver to assist me in loading my bike and panniers into the baggage area at the bottom of the bus. The doors to the baggage area always remind me of a DeLorean, the way they elevate open.

My phone buzzes, causing my whole purse to vibrate. I pull it out and look at the Caller ID. Nameless. Ignore.

The seat I choose for this Godforsaken bus trip is a window, on a lonely row. This allows me to stretch out my knee, place my purse and jacket under it for elevation, and top it with a bag of ice.

While I wallow in self-pity, the bus trip consists of a cascade of tears, sad music blasting through my headphones, and longing looks out the solo window.
Eventually the emotional drain of crying sends me to rest my eyes, and the two-hour bus trip to Hamilton flies by in my dream state.

Chapter Twenty-Seven

One Foot in Front of the Other

Much like Tauranga, I am scheduled for one night in Hamilton before I hit the road again. I came to the conclusion that I will stay in luxury again tonight. A decent hotel, equipped with a hot bath for soaking my knee and a warm bed to support my recovery. This trip has slowly morphed from shitting in bags to four-star plush pillow sets. My mountaineering friends would be disappointed; I am a little disappointed. But if a few nights of effortless rest are able to prepare me to finish the journey strong, then I will take them.

Tomorrow I will attempt to ride the last two sections of my trip. Originally I had planned to attempt the 146-kilometer motorway in just one day, biking my little heart out to finish the final leg into Auckland as strong as possible. However, given my recent accident, that plan has now changed. I will give myself more time for completion, taking two days and a night. This way I can spend my last night on the road in a tent. A fine way to end this journey.

To my surprise and delight, my knee is holding up well. I have a distinct feeling that sleeping in luxury and the hot bath really helped and allowed for the swelling to go down. Nightly applications of Tiger Balm didn't hurt either. The pain has almost completely subsided and the range of motion in my knee is normal enough to allow to me ride. With a sigh of relief after having checked the pressure on my tires and WD40'd my chain... off I go again!

The winding river path leads me out of Hamilton, providing a scenic view while avoiding the rush of traffic. This path takes me all the way out of the city limits and delivers me onto the motorway with a clear shot to Auckland. Four hours into the first day's ride, nice and slow, brings me to my stopping point at Te Kauwhata.

Tent setup takes place, per usual, but this time I am just off a road. A small patch of grass on the side of the river is all I can come up with as a place to pitch my tent. Unfortunately, being beside a road sketches me out a little bit. Firstly, I don't have anywhere to stash my bike, and in small towns like this one, teenagers are known to get into trouble. I know this because I used to be one of them here, rambunctious and loud, roaming the streets at night with no end in sight. Thankfully there are some relatively large flax bushes that line the wide river where I am able to hide my bike in the depth of the abundance of leaves.

This also provides my entertainment for the late afternoon. I cut a single strand of flax and sit on a bench that overlooks the river, as the sun begins its long evening routine of setting behind the earth's rotation. Stripping the flax into six thin parts, I begin to cross them, one over another, weaving a flax flower like I used to do as a child.

The orange light of the sun creates a reflection from the river, beautiful to my eyes.

Afterward I eat a simple noodle dinner, then crawl into my sleeping bag. I try to close my eyes, remembering that this is my final night of this incredible journey I have been on for the past 27 days. What a journey it has been. I am glad I did it solo. Glad I took the time alone on the road to process all the emotions and challenges that came with this adventure. The concept was simple—a girl on a bike, revisiting places from her own history. But it became so much more than just that; it became so much more than just me.

Feeling a little uneasy about sleeping right near a semi-main road, I pull my flip knife from my cooking set and place it by my pillow, which is composed of my jacket stuffed in the sleeping bag case.

I drift off to the thought that tomorrow may be the last morning that I get to appreciate the sun-kissed rays on my face, in the heart of New Zealand.

Chapter Twenty-Eight

Auckland Arrival

Waking to the sound of birds chirping and distant traffic from the motorway, I slowly open my eyes. Everything in my tent holds a mild smell of mildew; weeks' worth of unwashed clothes retaining my sweat from the long days of biking. My tent needs a good wash, my legs need to be shaved, my underarms are screaming for deodorant, and, at the same time, all seems right with the world….. except for the damn traffic messing with my tranquility.

My knee's swelling has definitely decreased; movement is far better than on previous days since the accident.

If all goes as planned, this will be my final five hours on my bike. The final stretch to Auckland as my journey comes to an end.

The mornings ride starts out strong, stronger than I expected it would, given the pain in my knee throughout the night. Back in Hamilton, I purchased a knee compression sock which served me well and has moderated the swelling.

On the way to Auckland, I begin to notice that what was once a fairly quiet main road with shoulders and plenty of open space is morphing into a fast-moving motorway, severely lacking in bike-friendly modifications. The rush of cars whirls me straight back to Highway Two out of Wellington, one of my least favorite sections of the trip so far. The constant stream of ongoing cars suggests I am not far from the city limits. Farm lands and animal pastures make way for shops and taller buildings.

Just as I am approaching a large bridge overpass, the harsh sound of a siren startles me. Next comes a muffled voice over a loud speaker.

"This is the police." *Ohhhhshiiittt!* "Please pull your bicycle over immediately!"

Should I make a run for it? I think to myself. I can't exactly hop the fence on the bridge. Something about cops makes me unnaturally nervous. Was I a convicted felon in a past life?

Pull over where? My thoughts are still racing. I'm as far over as I can possibly go and the traffic is millimeters away from splattering me like a tomato on a tennis racket. I hit the brakes and peer into my helmet's mirror, before turning my head in the most innocent way possible.

A police officer, dressed in a uniform that looks like he belonged on horseback in the 1940s, strolls toward my bike.

"What's the problem, officer?" I attempt to bat my eyelashes. Then I remind myself I am not 19 anymore, and no matter how I try to turn on my charm, there is no amount of eyelash-batting on the planet that can make me look cute in this miss-matched cycling outfit.

Damn, I think to myself, *I should have golf'd my way around New Zealand. At least those outfits are cute.*

"Ma'am, you are not allowed to bike on a motorway. I'm going to have to write you a ticket."

"Wait – what???" I blurt out in as much of an American accent as I can possibly put in two words. This is the one and only time my American accent may come in handy, and you best believe I will use it to an extreme.

"Yes, ma'am. It is highly illegal to cycle on a motorway."

"Oh. My. God. Seriously? I had no idea. I'm not from here and there's no, like signs, or anything!"

That's not quite true. I saw a sign awhile back saying no bicycles on the motorway, but there was no other way I knew of to take me straight into the city, so I chose to ignore the sign. My very last day on the motorway, after 28 days of cycling, and I am just now being pulled over. It could have been worse.

"Well, I suppose I could let you go just this once, but you are not allowed to cycle on the motorway. It is very, very dangerous."

"Thank you so much," I proclaim. "But I don't know how to get into Auckland without using the motorway."

"This road right down there." The officer points to the road passing under the motorway. "It will take you right into the city. Just stay straight on it, and you will be there in about an hour and a half."

"Thank you so much, officer." I turn my bike around and give him a friendly wave as I head toward the motorway exit.

Two hours later and the rush of traffic is still surrounding me. In the heart of Auckland, my cycle wheels head toward the home of a dear friend of mine, Mel. With Mel's wonderful friendship comes a warm shower and a queen-size bed. Pure heaven.

In the evening Mel and I head to the Auckland City Library, where I have a reading of my first book, *Journey of Heart: A Sojourn to K2*. We enter the building via the front entrance's large glass doors.

"Are you Sequoia?" an adorably nerdy man asks. I nod.

"These are for you." He hands me an exquisite green glass vase, filled to the brim with yellow tulips. "And this."

With a beaming smile on my face I take a small box from him. There is a note card that reads:

Big pat on the back.
Not all those who search are lost.
-   Rod

"Who is Rod?" Mel asks.

"A friend I met on the road." I say, opening the small box to reveal a silver necklace with a pendent of a girl carrying a knapsack.

"Holy fuck. That's a Karen Walker," Mel says.

"What's a Karen Walker?"

"She's an uber-famous Kiwi designer." We both gaze in admiration at the adorable necklace.

"You must have made quite an impression," Mel says with a wink.

I chuckle to myself as we head into the Library reading room. My mother is already there to greet me. Peter Hillary is also there, along with friends from different periods of my life in Aotearoa.

Chapter Twenty-Nine

Ghosts of Our Pasts

Much like David and Vicky, I first met Mel in the high hills of the Himalayas. It was as I was coming down from a climb that I was in a village called Lukla for the night. Lukla is the stopping point for the airport, and flights usually leave in the mornings, provided the weather is good. There are a number of small lodges that line the village, and as I arrived at the main entrance of one, I sat down and ordered a cup of Du Chia (hot milk tea). From the other side of the room came roaring voices that sounded like they were a couple-a-drinks in. I instantly picked up on the Kiwi accents, and, being the social butterfly that I am, made conversation with them. Turns out that the group of rambunctious Kiwis were a crew filming Sir John Kirwan's episode of a TV show that Mel was producing. Mel is the definition of a producer, fast-paced and creative, but still able to apply the analytical side of her brain. My kind of woman. Needless to say, that was the night that Sir John Kirwan, Mel, myself, and the film crew got rather intoxicated off Nepal's finest alcohol.

Since our fateful encounter in Nepal, my friendship with Mel has spanned many months and many emails. Like quite a few nomadic souls who have crossed my path over these last four years, Mel and I bonded over grief. A topic that very few are open enough to allow to be a connection to another who has also felt a similar pain. You see, Mel lost the love of her life, her sweet husband. Our conversations often start with "It's been a shit week" or "It hit me really hard the other day"—conversation points that we know one another can relate to and understand.

The reality of loss is that we no longer possess the physical connection to our loved one(s). The human connection that once existed is gone. But with that loss, we open ourselves up to a multitude of potential alternate connections. In my case, a series of individuals whom I otherwise might not have met or developed a relationship with. Mel is an ideal example of this outreach. She is a friend for life, raised from the hell of grief.

Mel, like myself, has spent the past few years in a whirlwind of travels. Many of which lead her to remote, fauna-filled destinations.

There is a reason individuals have a tendency to search for themselves in nature. Without this propensity, authors like Bill Bryson, Robin Davidson, or Cheryl Strayed would not be so wildly successful. Coming out of a physical and emotional journey like the one I just experienced evokes sensations that words fail.

I will say this… when setting a challenge for yourself, my recommendation is that you set your challenge in the heart of Mother Nature. There is a tranquility in nature, a tranquility that cannot be replicated. When we test ourselves, in the simplicities or in the extremes our world has to offer, we are awakening our soul. We are finding our solutions within our sense of self.

In the beginning …
If you asked why I chose to cycle New Zealand, I could not tell you.
If you asked why it took me so long to return to my homeland, I could not tell you.
If you asked how I dealt with the heartbreak of a great loss, I could not tell you.

But I can tell you now.

References

Robert Frost: *The Road Not Taken*
Kyle Dempster: *The Road from Karakol*
Interisland History Boards
Wellington Dock History Boards
NZHistory.govt.nz
GOOGLE
WIKIPEDIA

Thank You

Macpac
Natural High New Zealand
My dedicated editor, Jenny Meadows
My Dear Mother, Joanne Munisteri
Rod McGregor
Raphelle Andrews
Mel Rakena
Tamar Munch
Peter Hillary
David and Vicky Christie
Doris and Charlie Michaels
Denali Schmidt
Marty Schmidt

Printed in the USA
CPSIA information can be obtained
at www.ICGtesting.com
JSHW012012140824
68134JS00024B/2376